1000 HORRORS

THE MOST HORRIFIC BOOK EVER KNOWN

Gyles Brandreth
Illustrated by Terry Burton
A Carousel Book
Transworld Publishers Ltd

Other books by Gyles Brandreth

1000 QUESTIONS
1000 JOKES
1000 RIDDLES
1000 FACTS
1000 SECRETS
1000 TONGUE-TWISTERS
1000 BLUNDERS
CHALLENGE
SHADOW SHOWS
WHAT DO YOU KNOW?
THE BIG BOOK OF SECRETS
BRAIN-TEASERS AND MIND-BENDERS
THE BIG BOOK OF MAGIC
THE BIG BOOK OF PRACTICAL JOKES
THE BIG BOOK OF OPTICAL ILLUSIONS
CRAZY DAYS
THE CRAZY WORD BOOK
THE ENCYCLOPAEDIA

All published by Carousel Books Ltd.

1000 HORRORS THE MOST HORRIFIC BOOK EVER KNOWN
A CAROUSEL BOOK 0 552 542474

PRINTING HISTORY
Carousel Edition published 1983

Carousel Books are published by
Transworld Publishers Ltd.
Century House
61–63 Uxbridge Road
Ealing, London W.5.

Made and printed in Great Britain by the
Guernsey Press Co. Ltd., Guernsey, Channel Islands.

KEY

1. **Ghastly giggles**

2. **Horrible facts**

3. **Haunting horrors**

4. **Horror heroes**

5. **Practical horrors**

6. **Horror sound effects**

7. **Ghoulish games**

8. **Horror verse and worse**

9. **Human horrors**

10. **Witchcraft, customs & legends**

1000 HORRORS

THE MOST HORRIFIC BOOK EVER KNOWN

Britain has more ghosts per square mile than any other country in the world.

At Bracknell in Berkshire, the ghost of a policeman with a dreadfully mutilated face often roams the streets at night, causing people to faint in horror at his misshapen features.

 What did Count Dracula get after his first film?

Fang mail.

 On the Isle of Man, if someone was suspected of being a witch they were rolled down a hill inside a spiked barrel. If they died they were proved innocent, if they were still alive they were found guilty and put to death.

English witches were said to be able to **whistle up the wind**. At dawn the witches would face towards the direction they wished the wind to come from, and placing the first and fourth fingers of the right hand in their mouths, they would give three long, clear whistles to summon the wind.

A ghoul stood on the bridge one night,
Its lips were all a-quiver.
It gave a cough,
Its leg fell off
And floated down the river.

To make the sound of phantom horse's hooves, take two empty coconut shells and pierce a hole in the top of each. Tie a large knot at the end of a piece of string and thread it through one of the shells and back through the other. Knot the other end of the string securely. Holding on to the string, clip clop the coconut shells down a country lane one dark night.

Why do demons and ghouls get on so well?

Because demons are a ghoul's best friend.

What did the ghost say to the barman?

Do you serve spirits here?

Put a few drops of red ink onto a sheet of blotting paper. Allow them to dry and then cut them out. You now have little pools of blood that you can leave lying around.

 In the thirteenth century forty-two million people died as a result of the Black Death.

 Capesthorne Hall, Cheshire, is haunted by a number of spectres, the most frightening of which is a severed arm that gropes around a particular bedroom late at night.

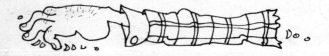

 One of the most famous vampires of all was **Count Dracula**, who is supposed to have lived in the fifteenth century in an ancient crumbling castle in Transylvania, now part of Romania. He also bought an abbey in England which he intended to use as a base for spreading vampirism.

What is Dracula's favourite society?

The Consumers' Association.

 On the roadside near Newmarket is the grave of a gipsy boy. The grave is always decked with fresh flowers, but nobody ever sees who places them there.

The Hound of the Baskervilles was the subject of a book by Sir Arthur Conan Doyle, and subsequently made into a film. The idea was based on a real creature called **Barguest**, who appears all over England often in the form of a hound, but can turn himself into other animals. His appearance is a warning of death or disaster.

A French actor called Pierre Messie could make his hair stand on end at will.

What do short-sighted ghosts wear?

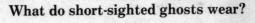

Spooktacles.

Loch Katrine, in Perthshire, Scotland, has a famous cave that is haunted by a wicked goblin. Children venturing inside the cave are never seen again.

'Ghostly Moans' is an ideal game for parties. One player is blindfolded, the rest arrange themselves in a circle around him. One of the players in the circle must let out a ghostly moan and it is the task of the blindfolded victim to identify who the ghost really is. If he guesses correctly the two change places and the game continues.

'Mummy, mummy, why can't we get a waste disposal?'

'Shut up and keep chewing.'

In 1348 eighty-eight cases of murder were recorded in Yorkshire. A modern equivalent in England and Wales would be not less than 10,000 a year.

Here lies returned to clay
Miss Arabella Young
Who on the twenty-first of May
Began to hold her tongue.

One of the greatest murder mysteries is that of Farmer John Dawson, a well-loved man with no enemies in the world. He was shot one Sunday evening for no apparent reason, a mystery that remains unsolved. Today his ghost searches for something in the hedge near where he was shot.

Many bridges in London have posts with stone balls on the top. These grisly pillars remain from the times when criminals were executed and their decapitated heads were placed on these posts. When this practice stopped the human skulls were replaced with stone balls.

In the lonely parts of Wales, of which there are many, hides a gigantic winged-toad called **Llamigan-y-dur** who feeds off sheep and leaps out of ponds dragging fishermen to their deaths.

As late as 1819 people could be hanged in Britain for cutting down a tree.

'Wolf children', who since birth have been brought up by wild animals, are never able to speak properly; they prefer to walk on all fours and dislike wearing clothes; they do not recognise their own image in a mirror and find it impossible to laugh.

Look for a picture of a skeleton in a book and play the game of **BONES**. If you are really clever you can set about naming every bone of the skeleton. If you prefer something easier, then cut out the skeleton very carefully and make a bones jigsaw. Cut the skeleton into pieces and try to put it back together again.

In the **Siamese Monster** game the players pretend to be joined to a partner at the forehead. You need an even number of players because it takes two players to make one monster. Four is the minimum number of players so that you can have two monsters racing against each other. To play the game the two players making the monster hold a ball or orange between their two foreheads, which means they have to press their heads together. The monsters line up in a row and at the command 'Go' they have to race to the opposite end of the room and back again. The first monster back is the winner. If the orange falls out it means the monster has lost an eye and cannot see where it is going, so it must start again.

Just before Christmas at Penryn in Cornwall, England, a ghostly coach drawn by headless horses appears. Local people believe that unless they turn their eyes away the ghostly coachman will spirit them away.

The **Bride of Frankenstein** was not the intended wife of the mad Doctor Frankenstein, but was intended for the monster himself. She was created out of the body of a girl called **Madeleine Ernestine**, but when she was brought to life she found the monster so ugly that she refused to marry him.

To make a ghastly clammy hand, fill an old rubber glove with cold water and tie the end securely so that none of the water will leak out. Paint the hand a flesh colour and leave it lying around.

What is big and green and sits in a corner all day?

The Incredible Sulk.

If you go to Italy, never kill a snake, for it is believed terrible things will happen to your family. The only safe time to kill a snake is during a full moon.

Mary Queen of Scots had a watch shaped like a skull, measuring three inches in diameter.

A cave on Wenlock Edge in Shropshire is said to be the tomb of a notorious outlaw called **Ippikin**. The cave was his secret headquarters during life and whilst hiding in the cave one day, a landslide blocked the entrance. If you stand today on these rocks and shout:

Ippikin, Ippikin,
Keep away with your long chin,

his ghost is said to appear and hurl you to your death on the rocks below.

13

On November 5th every year, a stone in the village of Shebbear, North Devon, known as the **Devil's Stone**, is turned as the church bells are rung to frighten away the Devil and prevent disaster befalling the villagers.

Burning at the stake was a legal execution in the USA as late as 1800.

Dab some blood-red paint over a crêpe bandage and allow it to dry. Wrap the bandage loosely around your neck. It will look as if your throat has been cut!

What do Devil's drink?

Demonade.

At Farringdon, Berkshire, beware of the headless ghost of Sir Robert Pye who walks by the north wall of the church.

CHEERS!

In July 1765 a cow gave birth to a calf that had two heads.

At Gatcombe Park, Gloucester, the home of Princess Anne, a huge black headless dog has been seen searching the lawns for some unknown phantom prey.

Gather together some lengths of chain, tie them on to a length of string and drag them along the ground to make the sound of ghostly phantom chains.

Glamis Castle, where Queen Elizabeth the Queen Mother spent much of her childhood, is said to house a monster so terrifying that only the Strathmore family know the true secret. The present Earl says: *'If you could only guess the nature of the secret you would go down on your knees and thank God it isn't yours.'*

The Grand Inquisitor, Peter Arbuez, although made a Saint in 1860, burned more than 40,000 people at the stake.

EXECUTIONER (To victim with head on the block): *'Sorry about this, but they do say third time lucky!'*

In the ruins of Hastings Castle, Sussex, rattling chains, ghostly music, and groans have been heard, and in the Autumn twilight the ghost of the murdered Thomas à Becket is often seen.

Fried mice — fried alive — used to be regarded in Britain as a cure for smallpox.

 In 1386 a pig was publicly hanged for killing a child.

What is Dracula's favourite slogan?
Please give blood generously.

 To give yourself a blood bath, put a few drops of cochineal or red food colouring in the water.

The guillotine was first used on April 25th, 1792, for the execution of a highwayman.

 At the Bank of England in London a number of people have seen an apparition known as the **Black Nun**, whose brother (an employee) was condemned to death for forgery. She still searches for him.

Lizzie Borden took an axe,
And gave her mother forty whacks.
When she saw what she had done
She gave her father forty-one.

 To produce the sound of rattling bones, take four pencils and hold them loosely in your hand and rattle them against each other.

A man pronounced dead in 1562 was buried. Six hours later his brother had a feeling that he might still be alive and the body was disinterred. The man was found to be alive and lived for another seventy-five years.

At Classenwell, on Dartmoor, there is a pool from which a legend goes that a voice comes from the pool at night and announces the name of the next person to die.

What do you call a kind-hearted, clean, handsome monster?

A failure.

At Boughton Hall in Surrey, England, the ghost of an elderly man smoking a pipe wanders up the stairs. The smell of his tobacco lingers on the air afterwards.

The monster King Kong was nearly twenty metres high.

'Doctor, doctor, I'm at death's door.'
'Don't worry, I'll soon pull you through!'

17

Mistress Sibell Penn, a nurse during the reign of Henry VIII, had a monument erected to her memory at Hampton Church. When it was removed in 1829 her spectre could be seen wandering around Hampton Court, and she could be heard spinning at her wheel. During later alterations to the palace a forgotten room was found. It contained a spinning wheel.

What do ghosts eat for dinner?

Spook-hetti.

Take a piece of orange peel, about a quarter of the orange, and cut it into fangs like this:

Wedge one piece under your top lip, and the other under your bottom lip so that they cover your own teeth.

It is calculated that there are approximately sixty-eight deaths a minute, 97,920 daily, and 35,740,800 annually in the world.

What monster is very unlucky?

The Luck Less Monster.

The writer, Nathaniel Hawthorne, used to visit the Atheneum Library in Boston daily and each day saw the Reverend Doctor Harris, a clergyman in his eighties, sitting in a chair by the fireplace reading. One day, after having seen Doctor Harris sitting in his usual chair, Hawthorne returned home to discover that the old man had died several days earlier. Hawthorne saw the old man sitting in his chair again the following day.

A drum belonging to Sir Francis Drake is said to roll unaided when England is in danger, a signal that its owner will return. It was heard just before the First World War.

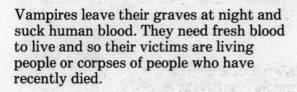

Vampires leave their graves at night and suck human blood. They need fresh blood to live and so their victims are living people or corpses of people who have recently died.

What is a skeleton?

Bones with the person off.

19

To dress up as a ghost all you need is an old white sheet, with a couple of holes for eyes so that you can see where you are going. Do get permission before you start cutting up sheets.

1st GHOST: *I find haunting this castle a real drag these days.*
2nd GHOST: *Me too. I just don't seem to be able to put any life into it.*

Miss Fanny Miles of Cincinnati, USA, had feet that were 60cms long.

Surgeons in Ancient Egypt had their hands cut off if their patients died.

A legendary hero of Ancient Rome was **Mucius**, a young man who resolved to murder the enemy, Porsensa, who was blockading Rome. Mucius was captured and sentenced to be burnt to death. Bravely he thrust his right hand into the fire and held it there without flinching. In admiration, Porsensa set him free. Mucius was from then onwards known as Scaevola — the left-handed.

20

NOT FAR NOW, MURPH!

Legend has it that the 4,000 year old circle of stones known as Stonehenge were magically transported to Salisbury Plain from Ireland by the **Wizard Merlin**.

 Balcomie Castle in Clackmannanshire, Scotland, is haunted by the ghost of a boy who starved to death 400 years ago. He was punished for whistling, and his eerie whistles can still be heard.

Why was the ghost arrested?

Because he hadn't got a haunting licence.

Listen to the eerie hoot of an owl and see if you can imitate it.

 'Mum, are you sure this is the way to make Pizza?'
'Shut up and get back in the oven.'

A gigantic prehistoric lizard called
Godzilla lived for thousands of years
undisturbed at the bottom of the Pacific
Ocean. It looked like a cross between a
dragon and a dinosaur, and a film about it
was first made in 1954 in Japan.

What do ghosts eat for breakfast?

Dreaded wheat.

Perfect examples of 'double
monsters' — two persons joined together,
but with distinct organs — were the
Hungarian sisters Helene and Judith the
South Carolina sisters Millie and
Christina (known as the 'two-headed
nightingale'), and the Bohemian sisters
Rosalie and Josepha.

In July 1765 a cow in Abergelly gave
birth to a calf which had two heads, four
eyes, four ears, two mouths, two tongues,
and two necks.

**What part of a dance do vampires like
best?**

The last vaults.

In Norfolk, England, every May 31st at
midnight a phantom coach sets out from
the village of Bastwick, driven by a mad
coachman. The coach appears to be on
fire, the passengers are all skeletons, and
it eventually crashes into a bridge and
plunges out of sight into the river.

A very young girl — call her Emma —
Was seized with a terrible tremor.
  She had swallowed a spider
  Which stung her inside her,
Gadzooks! What an awful dilemma!

 **What should you do if you find a green
monster in your garden?**

Wait until it ripens.

In 1740 a cow was found guilty of
witchcraft and hung on the gallows.

North-west of Bolton in Lancashire is one
of the oldest manor houses in Britain. It
is called Smithills Hall, and on one of the
doorsteps is the bloodstained footprint of
a man called **George Marsh**. Once a year
the footprint becomes deep red and wet.

Grasshoppers have white blood.

In 1650 the Oxford University Anatomy
Department acquired the body of **Anne
Green**, who had been hanged for murder.
Just as she was about to be cut open by
students, the body was found to be alive
and Anne Green fully recovered.

An epitaph in Bacton, Norfolk:

We	Must	All	Die
Must	We	Die	All
All	Die	We	Must
Die	All	Must	We

Which bears do ghouls like most?

Pall-bears.

The ghost of the Earl of Stratford appeared to King Charles I, warning the king not to take on Cromwell's forces at Naseby the next day. The king ignored the warning and was defeated.

In Turkey it is considered very unlucky indeed to step on a piece of bread on the ground.

To make yourself incredibly ugly, pad out your cheeks with cotton wool, ruffle up your hair so that it is really untidy, and then screw up your face as tightly as you can. Ugh!

The menacing cavalier of the '**Crab and Lobster Inn**', Sidlesham, Sussex, is a Cromwellian ghost who was hacked to death. A figure in a long cloak and tricorne is seen walking through the walls.

What happened to Frankenstein when he lost a hand?

He went to the second-hand shop.

A mad scientist called **Dr. Moreau** experimented with trying to turn animals into humans with horrifying results.

BUT MAVIS!

A tin tray or a piece of hardboard can be bent in such a way that it sounds like thunder.

The perfume Eau De Cologne was originally produced as a means of protection against the plague.

The ghost of **Catherine Howard**, the fifth wife of Henry VIII, is said to run screaming through the rooms at Hampton Court.

What is King Kong's favourite sandwich?

A godzilla cheese sandwich.

The monster Godzilla almost totally destroyed the huge city of Tokyo, crushing buildings like matchboxes.

In 1726 Charles Sanson, aged seven, inherited the post of **EXECUTIONER**.

The village of Pluckley in Kent is the most haunted village in Britain, with a red lady, a white lady, a phantom coach and horses, an old gypsy woman who was burned to death, and the ghost of a schoolmaster who hanged himself swings from a tree.

A horrible hairy wart can be made out of a little nose putty (which comes in sticks and can be modelled easily in your hands) with some hairs from a paintbrush stuck into it. It can be stuck to your skin using spirit gum.

There was a young fellow named Hall
Who fell in the spring in the fall.
'Twould have been a sad thing
If he died in the spring,
But he didn't — he died in the fall.

Which monster eats faster than any other?

The Goblin.

A pythoness is a witch and not a snake.

A particularly nasty ghost called the **grey man of Macdhui** haunts one of the highest mountains in The Cairngorms, Scotland. It is said to chase its victims, so don't make any attempts to meet it unless you have nerves of steel.

If you blow gently over the rim of a glass or jar you can produce the eerie sound of howling wind.

The word **'Abracadabra'** was originally a magic charm that was said to cure hay fever, although it is now associated with witches and wizards.

A hearse in America has the sinister registration number **U2**.

Why is Dracula a good guest to take out to dinner?

Because he eats necks to nothing.

Abbad El Motaddid of Seville used the skulls of his enemies as flower pots.

Traditionally the monster **Golem** was said to be made out of clay and resembled a human being, but could be magically brought to life. The only problem with a golem is that it grows bigger and bigger every day.

The Old Vicarage at Southwold in Suffolk is haunted by a ghost whose presence is accompanied by deep groans, heavy footsteps and the clanking of chains.

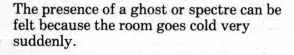

The presence of a ghost or spectre can be felt because the room goes cold very suddenly.

A witch's broomstick can be made by tying some twigs or straw around a stout stick.

In pagan times girls used to tie holly on to their beds to stop themselves turning into witches.

Bosworth Hall, Leicestershire, has a stain on the floor. It is of consecrated wine spilled by a priest 300 years ago, who knocked over his chalice whilst secretly celebrating mass. Cromwell's men knocked at the door and disturbed him. The stain is still damp.

Dried beans or peas can be attached to your face with spirit gum or copydex so that they look like ghastly warts or spots.

In 1969 black snow fell in Sweden.

Llewelly Peter James Maguire
Touched a live electric wire.
Back on his heels it sent him rocking,
His language, like the wire, was shocking.

What is the name of the overweight monster that lives at the Opera House?

The Fat-tum of the Opera.

London's Drury Lane Theatre, built in 1663, has seven phantoms haunting it.

Spiritualist **Amy MacPherson**, was buried with a live telephone in her coffin.

Cheshire witches used to stick pins in sheeps' hearts and small wax dummies when making curses.

What do ghosts like most about riding horses?

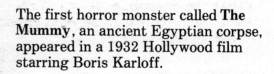

Ghoulloping.

The first horror monster called **The Mummy**, an ancient Egyptian corpse, appeared in a 1932 Hollywood film starring Boris Karloff.

When **Archbishop Cranmer** was burnt at the stake his heart was found intact amongst the ashes.

From some brown paper, cut out several bat shapes. Paint them black and hang them on pieces of cotton from the ceiling. To anyone walking into the room at dusk they will resemble real bats.

Fred Archer, a famous British jockey who died a century ago, haunts the racecourse at Newmarket. He rides a phantom horse which often scares many of the real horses there today.

Which day of the week do monsters like best?

Moanday.

 There is an undertaker in Los Angeles, U.S.A., called Ivor Coffin.

The planet Saturn is named after a very evil Roman God, who in mythology is said to have eaten all but one of his own children.

 Bettiscombe Manor in Dorset houses the skull of an eighteenth century West-Indian slave, which is alleged to scream if it is removed from the house.

Next time your dog howls, tape record the sounds. Then play it back very loudly so that it sounds like a werewolf.

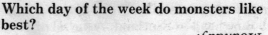

What did the headless horseman do when he lost his head?

He rode off to look for a headhunter.

 The poison cyanide can be produced from plumstones and applepips.

On January 13th an old fire ritual takes place at Burghead in Scotland. A barrel of tar is set alight, carried to the top of a hill and rolled down. If the man carrying the barrel up stumbles it means bad luck for the town. Pieces of tar picked up guard against witchcraft.

A giant moth called 'Mothra' or 'The Thing' appeared in a 1964 film called 'Godzilla vs. the Thing' in which it battled with the monster Godzilla. The monster moth won.

Why was Frankenstein so fond of the doctor that made him?

Because he kept him in stitches.

Bees die immediately they have stung someone.

The bomb went off too soon alas,
And here his story ceases.
The bits they found are buried here,
And so he Rests In Pieces.

St. Elian's Well in Llanelian on the Isle of Anglesey has the reputation of being an evil cursing well. To curse someone you inscribe their name on a pebble and toss it deep into the well with a pin.

The ugliest creatures in the sea are said to be the dugongs. They eat mainly seaweed, and the sight of them in the water led early sailors to believe that they were mermaids.

 At Glamis Castle centuries ago some members of a feuding Scottish clan were locked in a room and left to die. The screams of the dying men can still be heard. They died gnawing the flesh from their own arms. The room has since been bricked up so that nobody can ever see its grisly contents.

 During the reign of Elizabeth I, a monster dragon known as **Boa** was believed to slither around the countryside, sucking milk from cows before eating them whole.

Louis XIII of France was bled forty-seven times in one month.

What do you call a witch that goes on holiday to the sea, but never goes in the water?

A chicken sand witch.

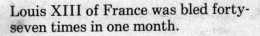

A method of execution in Mongolia was to nail the condemned into a coffin and leave him.

How do you raise a baby monster when you find one abandoned by its parents?

With a fork lift truck.

Burley Parish Church, Suffolk, occasionally echoes with organ music even though the church is locked and empty.

The Roman poet, **Virgil**, once spent £50,000 on the funeral of a pet fly.

Horror feet can be created by painting ugly blue veins onto stockings or tights.

The **Glaistig** was a Scottish monster that was half woman and half serpent that sucked the blood from young men.

To make a horror mask that will fit right over your head, blow up a balloon so that it is slightly larger than your head. Cut up 5cm square pieces of newspaper, dip them in paste and cover the balloon completely with four or five layers of paper. Leave the balloon in an airing cupboard for one week to dry. Pop the balloon and you'll be left with a shell. Cut around the base so that it will fit over your head, and cut out some eye-holes and nostrils. Decorate with paint, wool, or more papier-mâché.

The ghost of writer Emily Brontë appears each year on the date of her death, December 19th, at the Toby Jug restaurant in Howarth. Howarth was the home of the Brontë family and the parsonage where they lived can still be visited on the edge of the spooky Yorkshire moors of which Emily wrote in her classic novel *Wuthering Heights*.

An earnest young fisher named Fisher
Once fished from the edge of a fissure.
  A fish with a grin
  Pulled the fisherman in —
Now they're fishing the fissure for Fisher!

In the graveyard at Wesleton, Suffolk, is a gravestone called the **Witch's Stone** and a bare patch of ground over which no grass will grow.

How do skeletons eat meat?

In grave-y.

In Minehead, Somerset, the **'Whistling Spectre'** haunts the street. It is the ghost of **Widow Leaky** who whistles in a spine chilling way and has even been known to haunt ships at sea.

Practice a spine-chilling whistle in a way that you think the **'Whistling Spectre'** might be heard.

In the USA somebody dies of cancer every ninety seconds.

Netley Abbey in Hampshire has an underground passage that contains a secret so horrible that a man called Slown died of fright when he saw it. His last words were *'Block it up!'*.

In 1970 a man called **Roger Martinez** swallowed 225 live goldfish.

May Eve is known as **Beltane** or **Walpurgistnacht** and it is a night like Hallowe'en on which spirits and witches can be summoned. On this night the powers of evil are said to roam the earth from dusk to dawn.

Why did Frankenstein go to a psychiatrist?

Because he felt that everybody loved him.

At Westminster Abbey in London the ghost of a bloodstained soldier of the 1914 war has been seen near the tomb of the Unknown Warrior.

There was a young lady from Riga
Who rode with a smile on a tiger.
They returned from the ride
With the lady inside
And the smile on the face of the tiger.

In 543 AD bubonic plague swept through the world killing 10,000 people a day.

Gorgons were horrifying monsters that were like ugly women with hair made of live snakes. Anyone who looked upon them instantly turned to stone.

What should you do if you find yourself surrounded by Frankenstein, Dracula, the Wolfman, Golem, a couple of zombies and the Mummy?

Hope that it's a fancy dress party.

King John III of Poland was born, crowned and married on June 17th, and ironically died on June 17th too.

In August 1767 one Thomas Nicholson was hung for robbery and murder. His body swung on the gibbet for two winters and his bones were then buried on that spot at Beacon Edge Road, Penrith, Cumbria. Today people swear that the ghostly body can sometimes be seen still swinging at the end of the gallows and the rattling of his bones can be heard.

Hidden in ponds and rivers is said to be an old man with a long beard, known as **Nökk**. The monster-man lurks beneath the surface of the water waiting to drag young children down. So beware! Never go too close . . .

Giuseppe de Mai was born with two hearts.

There once was a chief of the Sioux,
Who into a gun barrel blioux
To see if 'twas loaded;
The gun it exploded —
As he should have known it would dioux!

**What do witches give their guests at
meal times?**

Pot-luck.

Black tooth enamel can be bought from
joke shops or theatrical costumiers. With
it you can black out your teeth and turn
yourself into a horrible old hag.

At St. Levan in Cornwall a phantom ship
mysteriously sails towards the shore and
disappears before reaching land.

The Romans were very fond of eating
dormice.

The river Ribble in Lancashire is haunted
by the spirit of Peg O'Nell, a servant girl
who was drowned by a witch. Peg, as the
spirit of the river, claims a human life
every seven years.

The **Sphinx** was a monster with the face of woman, the body of a lion, and the wings of a bird. She rested on a hill in Thebes, Egypt, and asked the riddle:

'Who is it that walks first on four feet, then on two feet, and finally on three feet?'

Until someone solved the riddle the Sphinx threated to plague Thebes. Do you know the answer?

Pelops, King of Pisa, was chopped up into little pieces by his father, **Tantalus**, and boiled.

A Norse method of saying farewell to their dead was to place the body on a boat, set fire to it and then push it slowly out to sea.

In German folklore a maiden called the **Lorelei** threw herself into the River Rhine in despair over a faithless lover. Today she haunts a rock on the right bank of the Rhine and sings, enticing sailors to their death.

In the year AD 1170, during the reign of Henry II, at St. Osythes in Essex, a real dragon said to be **'of marvellous bigness'** was witnessed burning down houses with its fiery breath.

40

Scandinavian witches, or trollwomen,
rode to their meeting places on the backs
of wolves bridled with snakes.

A fearful creature is the **Huckauf** or
Bogie Man who, superstition tells, will
jump upon your back as you walk along
the road at night. Watch out for the
Bogie Man!

A nightmare was thought by primitive
peoples to be a monstrous animal or
demon which would ride on sleeping
people, even to the point of death.

Why do mummies never tell secrets?

Because they like to keep things under wraps.

In the eighteenth century, a favourite
game for the boys of Westminster School
in London was that of stealing pieces of
skin and bone from the body of Queen
Catherine de Valois, whose shrivelled
corpse lay in an open coffin on display to
the public.

The female equivalant of a werewolf is called an **ESTRIE**. She can change her shape at will and has a gory appetite for children's blood. When an Estrie dies her mouth is filled with earth to prevent her doing evil again.

To make it look as if an arrow has gone right through your brain, get two thin pieces of dowling rod and a piece of wire.

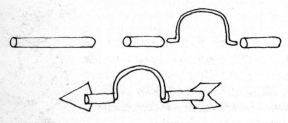

Bend the wire so that it fits over your head exactly. Now push each end of the wire into a piece of dowling. Finally stick a cardboard arrow tip and feathers on to the 'arrow', and wear it when you next walk down the street. Watch out for the Indians!

A human horror who has become a legend is **BLUEBEARD**. He murdered seven of his eight wives and kept their bodies in a locked room. His eighth wife managed to open the door one day and her gruesome discovery prevented her own untimely end.

Modern air-age gnome-like creatures known as **Gremlins** are blamed for any mechanical troubles that occur in aircrafts.

The Ancient Britons believed that the shadow of a person was part of their soul.

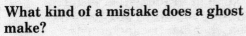

What kind of a mistake does a ghost make?

A boo-boo.

A fourteenth-century ghost known as the **Mad Monk** haunts a ruined chapel beside the golf course at Little Haldon, Devon. During his lifetime the Mad Monk persuaded weary travellers to enter his chapel, where he then robbed and murdered them, throwing their bodies down a well.

A Gaelic spirit whose wail warns of approaching death is known as a **BANSHEE**.

To play the **Banshee Game**, sit in a circle with your friends and take it in turns to wail like a Banshee. When each person has wailed, take it in turns to be blindfolded. When the player is blindfolded, the others must wail, one at a time, while the player tries to identify each Banshee from his or her wail. The winner is the one who gets most correct.

A fun party game is **'Hold Off the Body Snatchers'**. One person is chosen to be the body and another is the body snatcher. The remaining players form a circle around the 'body' whilst the Body Snatcher stands outside the ring. The object of the game is for the Body Snatcher to snatch the body by breaking through the circle. The players in the circle have to keep him away at all costs. The Body Snatcher can try and crawl under the locked arms or between the player's legs, or trick them and dart in when they are least expecting it. When the Body Snatcher succeeds, the two players who broke the circle then become the Body Snatcher and the Body.

To terrorize their enemies in the fifteenth century the Turks used a gun that fired half-ton stone balls. It took over a hundred men to manoeuvre the weapon.

Dr. William Price, a Victorian supporter of cremation, ordered that his body be burnt on a hill top in front of an audience. 20,000 spectators turned up to watch the event.

What do you call a nervous sorcerer?

A twitch.

Stirling Castle, like so many other castles in Scotland, is haunted. The ghost here is a pink lady, dressed in pink silk and followed by a pink light.

In 1978 a Tokyo gang leader, **Shoichi Murakamie**, was stabbed to death. To dispose of the body it was chopped into tiny pieces and put into a large pot of soup being cooked at a Chinese street market. More than fifty people unsuspectingly ate the soup.

In ancient Greece curses were scratched on to pieces of pottery or lead tablets and buried in the ground.

During the American Civil War, maggots were used to clean wounds by eating away the dead tissue.

Two brothers in Bermuda were killed while riding the same moped in the same street, by the same taxi driver in the same taxi with the same passenger — but one year apart.

A zealous locksmith died of late
And did arrive at heaven's gate.
He stood without and would not knock
Because he meant to pick the lock.

Choking is the sixth most common form of accidental death.

45

Why did the monster take his nose apart?

To see what made it run.

 The preview of the horror film **Macabre** was shown in an abandoned churchyard on a tombstone.

 Geryoneus was a Spanish king in classical mythology. Not only was he a giant that lived off human flesh, but he had three heads and six arms.

Where does a ghost train stop?

At a manifestation.

 Witches use bits of metal to cast spells. If you see a pin lying on the ground be sure to pick it up and put it somewhere safe. If you leave it there a witch might find it, which would be bad luck.

 See a pin and pick it up
And all day long you'll have good luck.
See a pin and let it lie,
And to good luck you'll say good-bye.

Which ghost was Emperor of France?

Napoleon Bones-apart.

In an awful 1958 horror film some ghastly monsters known as **The Brain Eaters** appeared. They were horrible insect-like creatures that attached themselves to the side of people's heads and . . . yes, you've guessed it . . . sucked out their brains.

Friday is said to be an unlucky day on which to be born, on which to be married, and you should never have your haircut, file your nails, or set out on a journey on a Friday.

If a friend has four joints in her fingers instead of three — watch out! — she is a witch!

Which monster makes strange noises in its throat?

A gargoyle.

At Bexley in Kent, Sir Thomas Atte Hall was gored to death by a wild stag. Having witnessed her husband's death, his wife, Lady Constance Hall, jumped to her death from a tower of their home. Ghostly screams now come from the tower and a woman in white is seen jumping from it.

 American gangster, Bugsy Siegel, developed a stomach puncture technique which caused corpses to sink when thrown into a river.

If you point at a grave your finger will rot away unless you stick it in the ground.

The **Matani tribe** of West Africa used to play football with a human skull.

Where do vampires collect their post?

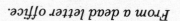
From a dead letter office.

In 1776 a woman who was very fond of sneezing, called Margaret Thompson, was buried in a coffin full of snuff.

The most famous monster of all, the **Loch Ness Monster**, is sighted on average twenty times a year. At least ten other Scottish lochs are said to contain monsters too.

The ghost of **Mad Maude**, a young nun burned at the stake 400 years ago, still haunts Weston on the Green in Oxfordshire. Her cries for help can still be heard.

What did the cannibal have for lunch?

Baked beings on toast.

Which monster comes down the chimney at Christmas?

Santa Claus.

Stage blood can be bought in bottles. It is a slow-running red liquid that can be used to great horror effect.

Tie three empty tin cans together to make the sound of ghostly clanking armour.

What is it called when demons parade through the street?

A demon-stration.

Christopher Lee was the greatest horror actor of all times and the most famous 'Dracula' of all. He was the first to show the bloodstained fangs of this Hammer horror vampire.

The bat is the only mammal that can fly.

OW YEAH!

A Roman method of torture was that of suspending their unfortunate victims from a great height by their thumbs.

In Africa a monster known as **Yena** digs up the graves of the dead and eats the remains.

At Strathpeffer in Scotland a woman suspected of being a warlock was burned in a barrel of boiling pitch.

Fourteen years before the sinking of the **Titanic** an incident in Morgan Robertson's novel **Futility** described the collision of a ship with an iceberg in the north Atlantic — the fictitious ship was on her maiden voyage and was called the **Titan**.

What do you flatten a ghost with?

A spirit level.

In the sixteenth century a man was born in China with transparent flesh.

French nun, Marie Lairre, was strangled at Borley Rectory and her bones were buried in the grounds. Her ghost haunted the Rectory for many years, until it mysteriously burned down in 1939. Onlookers watching the building burn could just distinguish a figure at one of the windows — it was that of a nun.

A game for those with strong nerves is **'The Murder Game'**. Sit everybody in a circle and put out all the lights so that the room is in total darkness. Now begin to tell a story about a gruesome murder. Say that the murderer began by gouging out the victim's eyes. You then pass around the circle two soft grapes. When they have been returned to you, continue the story. Say that next the murderer took out the victim's brain and pass around a wet sponge. Use your imagination and pass around suitable items. An ear can be cut out of a cabbage leaf, small carrots can be fingers, and so on.

Dover Castle in Kent is haunted by a headless drummer boy, murdered during the Napoleonic wars.

One of the most horrific monsters of all in Ireland is the **Fachan**. It has just one large eye in the middle of its forehead and a horrible scaley body. It lives off the flesh of people who travel late at night, so take care if you ever visit Ireland.

LITTLE BOY: *Mummy, what's a werewolf?*
MOTHER: *Be quiet and comb your face.*

Dr. Bell fell down the well
And broke his collar bone.
Doctors should attend the sick
And leave the well alone.

An extra eye in the middle of your forehead can be made from half a ping-pong ball, decorated with felt-tip pens to look like an eye, including lots of fine red lines so that it looks bloodshot. Flesh coloured plasticine can be used to make top and bottom eyelids, and to attach it to your forehead.

At Cater Common on Dartmoor a white phantom dog appears.

 In the 1961 film **Gorgo** a baby monster is captured and put on show. A gigantic monster, one of its parents, searches for its lost child, destroying much of London and terrorising the inhabitants as it does so.

 Hallowe'en was thought to be the one night in the year when the spirits of the dead were able to roam the earth, as well a witches. Many people light candles on this night (October 31st) to ward off evil spirits.

How do ghosts pass through a locked door?

They have a skeleton key.

 In Iraq you can eat snakes any day of the week except Sunday.

I had written to Aunt Maud
Who was on a trip abroad,
When I heard she'd died of cramp
Just too late to save the stamp.

One of the most notorious of all
Edinburgh's many ghosts is that of the
Devil who drives a coach pulled by
headless horses through the streets.

A very eerie sound can be made by
putting some uncooked rice into a box or
tin. Slowly tilt the box from side to side
and it sounds like the wind roaring.

Pierre Labellière had such a dislike of the
world that when he died he was buried
upside down.

What is a monster's favourite soup?

Scream of tomato.

A monster with a devil's head and a lion's
body was said to roam the English
countryside in the seventeenth century.
Called the **Wilde Beast**, it ate anyone who
went near it.

Paviland Caves in Glamorgan, Wales, are haunted by a **'Red Lady'** who died when trapped inside during a terrible thunderstorm. In 1823 a red-oxide stained skeleton was unearthed in the caves.

What jewels do ghosts wear?

Tomb stones.

The starfish is capable of turning its stomach inside out.

The only way to kill a werewolf is with a bullet or a dagger made from a silver crucifix.

Near Culloden House, Nairnshire, Scotland, besides the ghost of Bonny Prince Charlie a whole phantom army has been seen in the sky.

In 1877 Dr. Alpheus Meyers invented a **'tapeworm trap'**, which was similar to a mousetrap and was swallowed to catch the worm's head. Instead the patients usually choked to death.

In central America there is a fish which has four eyes.

To play the game of **'Body Snatchers'**, cut out as many pictures as you can from magazines of people. Stick the people on to card and then cut them up into six pieces — head, body, arms and legs. Shuffle all the pieces together and lay them face down on the floor. Players take it in turns to pick up a piece and the one to reconstruct a complete body is the winner.

To turn yourself into an old hag, sit in front of a mirror and screw up your face tightly. Using a stick of make up, draw in all the lines.

What did the barman say when the ghost asked for a drink?

'I'm sorry, but we don't serve spirits.'

At Marnhull in Wiltshire two ghosts cross Sackmore Lane carrying a coffin. Their faces are hidden.

Bells were originally tolled at funerals to ward off evil spirits.

Popular television monsters in America and Britain were a family called **the Munsters**. The father looked like Frankenstein's monster, the mother was a vampire, the son was a werewolf, and grandad was the splitting image of Count Dracula!

LITTLE BOY: *Mummy, what's a vampire?*
MOTHER: *Shut up and drink your soup before it clots.*

Henry VIII's second wife, Anne Boleyn, had an extra finger on her left hand.

At the home of the Sitwell family in Renishaw, Derbyshire, an elderly woman in a white cap haunts the bedrooms and people sleeping there have felt ghostly cold kisses on their cheeks. During alterations to the house an empty coffin was found under the floorboards.

Stage blood capsules can be bought from most joke shops. When you bite on them blood trickles from the corners of your mouth.

Willie had a purple monkey
Climbing up a yellow stick
And when he licked the paint all off
It made him deathly sick.

Why does a witch ride on a broom?

Because a vacuum cleaner is too heavy to fly.

At Hayne Manor on Dartmoor the appearance of a ghost with his head under his arm is said to fortell the death of the owner.

Lunan Barn in Scotland had a pond known as the **Witches Pool**. Witches were tried here by ducking.

A particularly unpleasant form of Roman torture was that of cutting off the victim's eyelids. He died, not from the wounds, but from insanity caused by lack of sleep.

To give yourself a forehead like Frankenstein's monster, use flesh coloured medicine or nose putty. Press it on to your forehead, covering your eyebrows to produce that familiar shape.

In the 1958 film **The Colossus of New York** a doctor built a robot and transplanted the brain of his own son into it. The monster he had created, called Colossus, then began terrorising people and was uncontrollable.

Where does Dracula get all his jokes?

From a crypt writer.

An American sailor once had a picture of a skeleton tattooed all over his body.

Czar Paul I was so conscious of being bald that anyone who mentioned it was immediately flogged to death.

Time wastes our bodies
And our wits;
But we waste Time,
So we are quits!

At the vicarage in Newark in the 1930's, the then vicar returned home one morning and on passing the window he saw a monk standing by the fireplace in his study. He hurried into the room by its only entrance. The room was empty.

In the seventh century the laird of the land in Tillicoultry was cursed by St. Serf for killing a ram. The curse said that no heir to the estate would enjoy owning it. In the next 200 years more than fourteen different families owned the estate unhappily.

1937 Hearse for Sale. Original body. Still in good condition.

Frederick the Great used to have his veins opened in battle to calm his nerves.

On 16 December 1897 William Terriss was stabbed to death by a mad actor outside the stage door of the Adelphi Theatre, and his ghost still haunts London although not at the theatre but Covent Garden Underground station. It has been seen in recent years and always in December.

In the village of Troo in France there is a speaking well.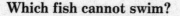

Why are vampires crazy?

Because they are often bats.

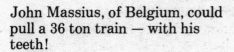

John Massius, of Belgium, could pull a 36 ton train — with his teeth!

Which fish cannot swim?

Dead ones.

Anne Griffith, one time owner of Burton Agnes Hall in Yorkshire, was attacked by robbers and fatally wounded. On her deathbed she requested that after her death her head remain in the Hall. At first her request was not kept, but the house became filled with screams and noises of horror, and so after a few weeks her head was brought back and sealed inside one of the walls where it remains to this day.

In Llanelian, Wales, there is a cursing well which has a reputation of horror. To curse someone you write their name on a pebble and throw it into the well.

To make a horror mask, make a model the same size of your face out of plasticine. Cover it with papier-mâché and leave it to dry for about a week. Remove the plasticine and paint the mask so that it looks like a demon or vampire.

On the anniversary of her execution, 19th May, Anne Boleyn haunts her birthplace — Blickling Hall in Norfolk. Just before midnight she arrives in a black coach, drawn by four headless horses and driven by a headless coachman. Anne leaves the coach, carrying her own detached head in her hands.

To make the eerie sound of rain, drop some grains of rice from a height, one at a time on to a tin tray.

A very bloodthirsty monster was the **Minotaur** which was half man and half bull and ate seven boys and seven girls every year. The monster lived in a maze which if anyone entered they could never find their way out.

Archbishop Hatto II of Germany, who cruelly put people to death, was himself attacked by hordes of rats and was eaten alive.

In the 1880's it was possible to buy two dozen live frogs for two shillings (ten pence).

What did the father ghost say to his son?

'Spook only when you are spooken to.'

During dinner at the Ritz
Father kept on having fits.
And, which made my sorrow greater,
I was left to tip the waiter.

It might be advisable to avoid Devon roads at night as you might meet seventeenth century murderess, Lady Howard riding in a coach of bones drawn by headless horses complete with headless coachman.

One of the most elusive monsters is the **Abominable Snowman** or **Yeti**. Although it has been seen on occasions by mountain climbers, the only real evidence of its existence are the gigantic footprints 33cm by 46cm which it leaves in the snow.

When making a monster mask stick on macaroni for teeth to make it look even more realistic and frightening.

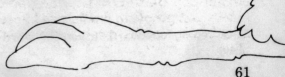

'Find the Charm' is a good game for vampires and werewolfs to play. A curtain ring is the charm and it is threaded onto a long loop of string. One player is chosen to be the vampire and stands in the middle of the circle of string. The other players stand around him in a circle with their two hands gripped over the string. They must try and move the charm around the string from person to person without it being spotted.

What happened to the two blood cells?

They loved in vein!

Epitaph:

Affliction sore long time he bore,
Physicians were in vain!
Grown blind, alas! He'd
Some Prussic Acid,
And that put him out of his pain!

The French Empress and wife of Napoleon, Marie Louise, could move her ears at will and even turn them inside out.

'Evil' spelt backwards gives the word 'Live'.

Buhram, a member of the violent **Indian Thugee Sect**, strangled over 900 people in fifty years.

Touching wood for luck was an early Christian practice, for wood is symbolic of the cross. To stab a vampire through the heart with a stake is therefore a triumph of good over evil.

What is a monster's final drink?

His bier.

Many insects, such as locusts, grasshoppers and ants, are eaten as special delicacies around the world.

Monsters are not all animals. Sometimes they are plants. The Triffids, created by writer John Wyndham in his book **The Day of the Triffids**, were huge plants which had minds of their own. They could move around and sting people to death.

At Lyme Park, Cheshire, a phantom funeral procession has been seen. The coffin is followed by a woman in white. It is said to be the funeral procession of one Sir Piers Legh who died in 1422.

'It is the same old game,' she said
'So play it how you like, my dear.'

'This time it's not the same,' he said,
Slitting her throat from ear to ear.

What is Dracula's favourite song?

'Fangs for the memory.'

Practice making monster shadows on to a blank wall by positioning yourself in front of a torch or lamp. Your hands can produce all kinds of gruesome shadows.

At Bradford Pool on Dartmoor is said to be a ghost who lures anyone going too close to a certain death.

Above the church door at Stoke Dry in Rutland a vicar once imprisoned a witch in the porch and starved her to death. Her spirit is still felt there.

A grasshopper's legs can walk on their own, even when detached from the body.

Greek historians record that **Aeschylus** died after being hit on the head by a tortoise which had been dropped by an eagle flying overhead.

A bird, a man, a loaded gun.
No bird. Dead man. Thy will be done.

      (Anon)

 In 1921 an army officer was riding along the road between Postbridge and Two Bridges on Dartmoor when a pair of hairy hands grabbed hold of him and pulled him off his motorcycle.

 If you would like to see a weird and wonderful collection of items, visit the **Witchcraft Museum** in Boscastle, Cornwall.

What do you find in a haunted cellar?

Whines and spirits.

 Janus was a Roman God. He had two faces. One which was sad and looking back on the past, the other happy and looking to the future. You can turn yourself into Janus by making two masks and putting one on your face, the other on the back of your head.

To give yourself four horrible faces, simply find a cardboard box that will fit over your head and paint a demonic face on each of the four sides.

 Attendant in the Chamber of Horrors: *'Kindly keep your wife moving, sir, we're stock-taking.'*

65

A hairy two-headed monster was the star of a 1962 Japanese horror film called **The Manster**.

Knock, knock.
Who's there?
Frank.
Frank who?
Frankenstein, of course!

A method of suicide in China used to be to eat half a kilo of salt.

In the sixteenth century witches could be distinguished by their habit of throwing back their hair, an inability to cry and their habit of walking backwards intertwining their fingers.

An anagram of '**funeral**' is '**real fun**'.

After Sir Walter Raleigh was executed in 1618, his widow had his head embalmed and kept it in a red leather bag, which she carried with her everywhere until her death in 1647.

What's the difference between a wizard and the letters K, E, M, A, S?

One makes spells the other spells makes.

66

In the Middle Ages a monster known as **Gulon** devoured human corpses. It is now extinct. Thankfully!

Nobody loves me, everybody hates me
I'm going in the garden to eat worms.
Long slim slimy ones,
Short fat fuzzy ones,
Gooey — ooey — ooey ones.
The long slim slimy ones slip down easily,
The short fat fuzzy ones stick to your
teeth,
And make you go er er yum yum.

On the anniversary of his death, 26th February, the ghostly footsteps of Sir Christopher Wren can be heard climbing the stairs at Old Court House in Middlesex.

What is a skeleton's favourite pop group?

Boney M.

Frankenstein's monster was originally very kind and longed to be loved by everyone, but because everyone was horrified by his appearance he was rejected and so he began a reign of terror.

When disguising yourself as Dracula do not paint your lips red, but use make-up to paint them black.

67

The murder rate in medieval England was twenty-six times greater than it is today.

 Lady Elizabeth Hoby of Bisham Abbey who died in 1609 has haunted her former home ever since. She felt that education was so important that she beat her children if they did badly in their studies. On one occasion she locked one of her sons in his room to finish his work, and was called away. She forgot to tell the servants he was there and when she returned he was dead with his tear-stained head resting on his books. Lady Hoby never forgave herself and her wails are still heard to this day. Alterations to the abbey in the nineteenth century brought to light some copy books that had been hidden for centuries. One of the pages was blotted as if by tears. . . .

 What did the skeleton reply when the bus driver called 'Fares please'?

'Sorry, I'm skint.'

Find a door in your house that needs some oil on the hinges. Open and close it very slowly and see if you can make a horror creaking sound.

In all the films and books about Frankenstein's monster, nobody has ever been able to kill him. This means that he he still around. But who knows where . . .

In 1599 James I wrote a book about Witchcraft which he called **Daemonologie**.

In 1610 a Polish Countess called Elizabeth Bathory murdered 650 young girls in order to bathe in their warm blood, which she believed would renew her youth.

What menaces the deep and plays the banjo?

Jaws Formby.

The guillotine was said by its inventor, Dr. Guillotine, to be a painless form of execution and that the victim felt nothing more than a chill on the back of the neck. We cannot tell how he knew this for no victim could ever explain how it felt!

*Hickory dickory dock
Three mice ran up the clock.
The clock struck one . . .
The other two got away with
minor injuries!*

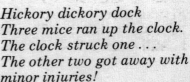

At Horseheath in Cambridgeshire a ghost who buried some gold is said to haunt Money Lane. When there is a full moon his voice is heard to say: *'Take up your spade and follow me.'* Nobody ever does. They could end up digging their own grave.

A witch's book of magic spells and curses is handed down from generation to generation. Each new generation copies out the book by hand and then destroys the original.

There was a young cannibal called Ned
Who used to eat onions in bed.
His mother said, 'Sonny
It's not very funny
Why don't you eat people instead?'

If a monster is born in Turkey, grows up in Ireland, spends twenty years terrorising people in Britain, and then dies in America, what is he?

Dead.

King Gustav III of Sweden thought that coffee was poisonous and condemned a criminal to drink it until he died. The man lived to be 83!

Spiders are used in the manufacture of anaesthetics.

In the horror film **The Devil Bat** a mad scientist created monster vampire bats that sucked blood from any man wearing a special aftershave lotion. The scientist eventually spilt some aftershave lotion on himself. You can guess the result!

When making yourself up to look like a monster, don't forget to pad out your cheeks with cotton wool for a greater horror effect.

North Road Station, Darlington, Durham, is haunted by a Victorian station clerk who committed suicide there in 1890. He once appeared to a nightwatchman there who took a swing at him, and hit his knuckles against the wall after they had passed right through the ghost.

Why did Henry VIII have so many wives?

Because he liked to chop and change.

The actress Sarah Bernhardt frequently used to sleep in a rosewood coffin.

During the Dissolution of the Monastries in the sixteenth century, the bells of Whitby Abbey were removed and were to be taken by boat to London. Although the water was calm, the boat carrying the bells sank for no reason. The bells can sometimes be heard ringing under the sea.

 Up until 1905 criminals in China used to be branded with a hot iron.

In Tudor times, to see if a man was guilty of a crime he was made to carry a red hot metal rod in his hand. If his hand did not blister he was said to be innocent.

There was a young man from Bengal
Who went to a fancy dress ball.
He decided to risk it
And went as a biscuit
But a dog ate him up in the hall.

 What is a viper's favourite football team?

Slitherpool.

72

Ghostly footsteps and the sound of something being dragged across the floor can be heard in the middle of the night at the Manor House in Flansham, Sussex.

A fourteenth-century Serbian prince called **Marks Kralyeric** is said to have killed 1000 Turkish soldiers with a sword 1.82m (6ft) long and weighing 22.6kg (50 lbs).

When making yourself up to look like Count Dracula use make-up to make your skin white like a corpse.

To make the sound of a large old log fire crackling in a grate, such as might be found in a haunted manor house, gather two or three friends together and all click and snap your fingers together in succession. It will sound just like logs crackling.

What is an undertaker's most unfavourite motto?

'Never say die.'

Epitaph
Here lies a chump who got no gain
From jumping on a moving train.
Banana skins on platform seven
Ensured his terminus was Heaven.

The **Demon Manchanda** is a monster with two heads and two bodies, four feet, two forked tails, and horns, rather like a double demon. Not anything you would wish to meet!

During the wedding breakfast of Alexander III of Scotland at Jedburgh Castle a shrouded and masked figure appeared. The shroud and mask were torn off the figure to reveal **nothing** inside.

A frog can jump twelve times its own length.

 The sound of an eerie clock ticking can be made by tapping a stick on a hollow wooden block.

Amongst the witches on Hallowe'en in Scotland walks the figure of **Green Lady Jean**. She was deserted by the man she loved and was told by a witch to wear fairy clothes of green. To obtain these she was told to sit all night on the 'Corbie's Stane'. This she did . . . and died.

What kind of meat did Dracula hate?

Steak (Stake).

The spectral figures of a woman with eyeless sockets and a tall priest haunt an old mill near Newcastle-Upon-Tyne. It is said that the woman committed suicide after the priest refused to hear her confession of murder.

In 1883 a Chinese priest in Shanghai decided to grow his fingernails; twenty-seven years later they were 58cms (22.8 ins) long.

A ghost known as '**The White Lady of Wolterton**' is said to be the spirit of one Lady Scamler, whose family tombs were destroyed. The ghost now searches the ruined church for her own tombstone and resting place.

Lieutenant Erika Uehlinger was dismissed from the United States Air Force because she claimed to be a witch.

A medieval game that was played on All Hallow's Eve is one that is no longer played today, and for good reason too. The players hung a stick horizontally from the ceiling with a length of string. On one end of the stick was an apple and on the other a candle. The object of the game was to twirl the stick rapidly and the medieval merrymakers had to jump up and catch the apple in their teeth. In most cases they either scorched their faces or ended up covered in hot wax. Which is one reason why the game is definitely not played today!

An ancient custom on Hallowe'en was that of eating an apple in front of a mirror. It was said that the person you would marry could be seen peering over your shoulder.

The above custom is reflected in this ancient rhyme:
Wee Jenny to her granny says:
'Will ye go wi me, granny?
I'll eat the apple at the glass
I got frae Uncle Johnny.'

Why did Dracula carry his coffin with him?

Because his life was at stake.

The monster-sized giant squid has eyes 275mm across.

How do undertakers calculate the cost of a funeral?

By dead reckoning.

 At the end of the last century a number of human horrors were displayed at fairgrounds. One such man was under 3ft tall and was billed as a Fairy Child that 'never speaks. It has no teeth, but is the most hungry and voracious creature in the world . . .'

The word '**warlock**' comes from the Old English **waer** meaning '**truth**' and **leogan** which means '**to lie**', and originally meant an oath-breaker or traitor. By 1460 it meant the male equivalant of '**witch**'.

Children born on Hallowe'en are believed to possess special mystical powers and can communicate with spirits.

Snakes are creatures of ill-omen. To prevent yourself getting bitten it is said that you should carry a stick made of ash and wear a circlet of ash twigs in your hair.

 'Now, Sonny, tell me where you've buried your dad in the sand. He's got the train tickets home.'

77

In 1878 a Chinese newspaper contained an article revealing that young children were often stolen as babies and placed in a vase with just their heads outside. They were kept for years sitting in these vases, carefully fed and looked after, until they reached the age of twenty when they were taken into a wood and 'discovered' and later displayed as wild-men at fairgrounds.

Ballindaloch Castle in Scotland is haunted by a Green Lady who appears nightly.

MRS. MONSTERS: *I don't know what to get my husband for Christmas.*
FRIEND: *Do the same as I did for mine, get him four pairs of gloves for his hands.*

To make the noise of rats scratching away, get an empty shoe box and scratch your finger nail along the top.

 An ancient Hallowe'en game was to tie several apples on to a piece of string and twirl it around. Whoever's apple falls off first will be the first person to marry.

 A seventeenth century remedy for snake bites was to thrust your hand into the stomach of a freshly killed chicken and keep it there until the chicken was cold. If its flesh turned black it meant that the snake poison was out of your body.

A fifteenth century hunchback bellringer of Notre-Dame cathedral was **Quasimodo** — otherwise known as **The Hunchback of Notre-Dame**. He was portrayed in a number of films, the most famous was Lon Chaney's version in 1923.

At the church in Castor, Lincolnshire, a ghostly monk plays the organ during the night.

Blossom on an apple tree in Autumn is said to be an ill omen:
'A bloom on the tree when the apples are ripe
Is a sure termination of somebody's life.'

At the top of Dragon Hill in Berkshire is a grassless patch of ground. According to tradition, St. George fought the dragon on this hill and the monster's blood spilled out and poisoned the ground.

What did the modern undertaker call his funeral parlour?

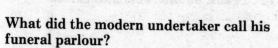

The departure lounge.

Strange though it may sound, at Long Wittenham in Berkshire the local Co-op is the scene of poltergeist manifestations.

In Greek mythology a two-headed dog monster called **Orthos** was said to guard the cattle of Geryon, a three-bodied giant. Orthos was killed by the hero Hercules.

There was an old man of Vancouver
Whose wife got sucked into the hoover.
He said, 'There's some doubt
If she's more in than out
But whichever it is, I can't move her.'

The human brain is four-fifths water.

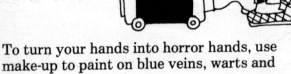

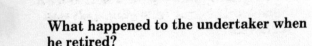

To turn your hands into horror hands, use make-up to paint on blue veins, warts and scars.

What happened to the undertaker when he retired?

He went and buried himself in the country.

On the Isle of Man it is believed that witches can transform themselves into bats and enter houses in this form.

80

Many breeds of tropical fish could survive in a tank of human blood.

In Oxfordshire, if a bat flies around a house three times it is thought to be an ill omen.

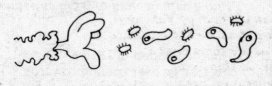

 In Siberia being pelted by lice and slugs means '**I love you**'.

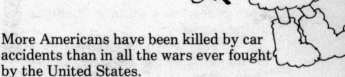

More Americans have been killed by car accidents than in all the wars ever fought by the United States.

An ancient witches' spell to detect an enemy was this:
A length of scarlet yarn was tied with nine knots as the following spell was chanted:

> *These knots I knot,*
> *To know the thing,*
> *I know not yet,*
> *That I may see*
> *The one who is my enemy.*

The yean was then placed under the witch's pillow and it was said that in her dreams she would see anyone who meant her harm.

Why did Dracula keep his coffin in a vault?

Because he liked to have vaulty winks.
(Forty winks)

At the Tower of London in 1816 a sentry on duty saw a large bear coming towards him. He struck at it with his bayonet, but the weapon went right through the creature without harming it.

Ooey gooey was a worm, a wondrous worm was he.
He stepped upon a railway line, the train he did not see.
Ooey gooey.

A superstition is that if three people take part in the making of one bed, someone will die in it within the year.

The novelist Robert Louis Stevenson created that strange man with two characters, **Dr. Jeckyll and Mr. Hyde**. The evil Dr. Jeckyll commits ghastly murders throughout London, but eventually destroys himself.

Until less than one hundred years ago corpses waiting to be buried were kept in the cellars of public houses.

'My husband wants me to get him something electrical for his birthday.'
'How about an electric chair?'

At Newton-le-Willows in Lancashire the ghosts of Royalists who were caught and hanged by Cromwell in 1648 can still be heard marching to their doom.

John Merrick, the **Elephant Man**, has been called one of the ugliest men who ever lived. He had a massively distorted head and many characteristics of an elephant giving the grotesque appearance of a man who had been half changed into an animal.

In the eighteenth century church bells were pealed to protect people from the 'shadow of phantoms'.

It was once believed that a witch's power could be broken by drawing some of his or her blood. A common practice was to try and scratch a witch between her nose and mouth or 'above her breath.'

FIRST GHOST: *I don't seem to frighten people anymore.*
SECOND GHOST: *No, we might as well be dead for all they care.*

In 1349 near Chipping Norton there was found a 2-headed serpent that had the faces of women and huge wings like a bat.

In 1821 one John Davies of Montgomery in Wales was wrongfully hanged for theft. Before he died he prayed that God would prevent grass growing on his grave as a sign of his innocence. Today a bare patch in the shape of a cross on which no grass will grow can be seen on his grave.

In Greek mythology a monster serpent with a hundred heads that never went to sleep was called **Ladon** or the 'everwatchful dragon'. The monster guarded a tree bearing golden apples, and was eventually killed by Hercules.

Dionysus, the Tyrant of Heraclea, had sharp needles inserted in his chairbacks to prevent himself from falling asleep. He was so fat that if he had dropped asleep in a chair he would have suffocated himself.

 In Italy the date November 2nd is celebrated as the 'Day of the Dead'. On this day everyone visits the graves of their dead relatives to lay flowers and light candles.

Little Miss Muffet
Sat on her tuffet
Eating her Irish stew.
Along came a spider
And sat down beside her
So she ate him up too.

In the Middle Ages a cure for leprosy was to stand under the gallows and allow the hanged man's blood to drip on you.

Oxney Court in Kent is haunted by the ghost of a lady in a dark grey coat, she is frequently seen by the roadside and a busdriver once stopped to pick her up. The lady disappeared.

A 17th century cure for epilepsy was to take a small quantity of grated skull with your food. It had to be the skull of somebody who had committed suicide.

VAMPIRE WIFE: *Dracula, dear, as we are going on holiday tomorrow, remind me to tell the blood man to stop leaving the daily pinta.*

On 8th February 1855 the Devil visited Devon, leaving a 100 mile trail of cloven hoof prints in the snow. The tracks revealed that it was a creature that walked on its hind legs and the prints were unlike those of any known living creature.

The Roman Emperor Claudius was once given a present of a real giant. The Emperor of Arabia gave him a man called **Gabbaras** who was 9 feet 5 inches tall.

In the depths of Llyn Cowlyd in Caernarvonshire is said to lurk the Welsh equivalent of the Loch Ness Monster.

At Tidmarsh in Berkshire on clear nights with a full moon the ghost of a drowned boy is seen rising from the waters of a stream near the old rectory.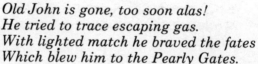

Old John is gone, too soon alas!
He tried to trace escaping gas.
With lighted match he braved the fates
Which blew him to the Pearly Gates.

To make a hairy monster mask like King
Kong, make a papier-mâché mask by
pasting newspaper on to a balloon and
allowing it to dry. Cut the dried ball in
half and you will have the bases for two
masks. For a hairy monster, cover the
mask hairy string such as hemp which
you can fluff up with a steel comb.

To make an eerie howling sound, place an
old violin on a table. Tie one end of a piece
of string to the door handle, and the other
end to a weight. Hang the string over the
violin strings so that when someone
opens the door the string will move
against the violin with a screech.

If someone from the Lugabra tribe in
Uganda is injured he goes to the graves
of his dead ancestors and invokes their
aid in getting his revenge.

If a clock strikes thirteen it is said to
fortell a death.

During a thunderstorm it is said that a
pack of bloodthirsty hounds set out on
hunting expeditions across the sky, which
are supposedly the souls of unbaptised
children.

What do you get if you cross a skeleton
with a packet of crisps?

Snacks that go crunch in the night!

Rait Castle, Nairnshire, Scotland is haunted by a handless girl in a bloodstained dress. It is the spirit of a girl who fell in love with a boy from a rival Scottish clan. Because of her betrayal, the Chief of her own clan chopped off her hands.

 Which is the scariest cheese?

Muenster!

 Evidence of witchcraft in London was unearthed in 1904 when during street excavations a brown jug was discovered containing a cloth heart stuck with pins, some human hair and nail parings. Obviously this was a spell to cause pain or injury to someone.

'Siamese Twins' are two people that since birth have been joined together. Usually they are joined side by side, but one unfortunate pair of twins in America were born joined in such a way that the stomach of one was attached to the other twin at the small of his back. The one in front could never see who he carried behind him, and the one behind spent his life gazing at the back of the other's neck.

Marwell Hall in Hampshire is haunted by Jane Seymour, third wife of Henry VIII, who died giving birth to Edward VI.

Where does a 500 pound monster sleep?

Anywhere he wants to!

A horror game that is great fun to play is **'Prisoners of the Tomb'**. Two players have ventured into the dark tomb which is guarded by a monster who has trapped them inside. Only one person has a chance to escape. Two players are blindfolded. The person pretending to be the monster makes a moaning noise and says: 'Mortal men your time has come, find the keys or die,' and throws a bunch of keys on the ground. The first of the two players (blindfolded) to find the keys is spared and scores one point. The other goes on to become the monster.

On 12th July, 1961, the citizens of Shreveport, Louisiana, ran for their lives when the sky turned black and it rained **green peaches!**

The sight of a dog rolling on the ground; the sound of a wolf howling; birds fleeing from the sea; or finches or sparrows chirping at dawn were all considered by witches to be signs that a storm was brewing.

A dead man's hand was once thought to have curative powers. People in the seventeenth century frequently visited the gallows to be cured of their ailments by touching a dead man's hand.

A popular superstition is that of breaking up an empty egg shell to prevent witches using them as a means of transport. In 1673 during the trial of Anne Baites for witchcraft, a witness said he had often seen her travelling this way.

Number 45 Quarry Road, Winchester, has no less than three ghosts, including a man in black, a lady in white and a nun. Curtains have been drawn by unseen hands and the smell of something dead lingers in the air.

What does a monster say when he steps on a Devil's tail?

'This is the end!'

In 1925 the actor Lon Chaney created the horribly disfigured monster **The Phantom of the Opera**, who wears a mask and lives in the cellars of the Paris Opera House. He embarks on a reign of terror in revenge for his horrible looks.

In 1360 more knights were killed by lightning than were killed in battle.

 In the nineteenth century Frank Lentini found fame because he was born with three legs. He used to be very good at playing football!

 Mr. Window Cleaner, you'll soon be well
After all, it wasn't far you fell.
You certainly received a nasty crack.
Don't worry though you'll get your ladder
back.

A Dracula cape can be made from a semi-circle of black material, with the straight edge about 150 cm long. In the middle of the straight edge cut a smaller semi-circle to fit the back of your neck. Stitch some black ribbon to this edge so that you can tie the cape around your neck, and you will be all set to become a vampire. Wear the cape with black trousers, white shirt and black bow-tie to dress just like Count Dracula.

In Denmark, Germany and Iceland, anyone with eyebrows that meet in the middle is suspected of being a werewolf.

In the fifteenth century witches were believed to have the power, with the Devil's assistance, to change their shapes and take animal forms.

What do you get if you cross a monster with a rose?

I don't know, but I wouldn't try smelling it!

Dunwood Farm in Herefordshire is haunted by '**Old Gregg**', who was poisoned by being given stewed toad for supper.

In Wales a monster that is half horse and half man, called **Afanc**, is believed to live in mountain pools and is almost impossible to kill.

In various countries throughout the world insects are eaten as a delicacy. The most popular are: ants, locusts, grasshoppers, beetles and caterpillars.

Zombies are strange monsters that look just like living people, and they were once living people, but now they are the walking dead. Their faces are drained of blood. Their eyes have a frightening stare, they never speak, they never blink and never seem to breathe.

To make yourself look like a zombie, comb your hair right back from your face, cover your entire face and lips with white powder and make-up. Use grey eyeshadow to put dark rings around your eyes, and put a little just under your cheek bones to give your face a thin, hollow look. Wear old clothes so that you look as if you have just crawled out of a grave. Practice a zombie-like stare and you will look like one of the walking dead.

To leave a grave open over a Sunday is an ill-omen. The grave is said to yawn for another corpse.

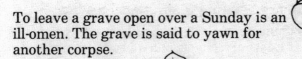

Ripley Castle in Yorkshire is haunted by a nun who knocks on bedroom doors, but only enters if the occupant shouts: '*Come in!*'

Kittens born in May were once considered very unlucky and were drowned for no better reason than the date of their birth.

93

A test for witchcraft was to drive a nail into the suspected person's footprint. If the person was a witch they would be forced to return and remove the nail.

How do you keep from dying?

Stay in the living room.

In a 1957 film called **Attack of the Crab Monsters**, an island in the Pacific became overrun with gigantic monster crabs whose main source of food was human heads.

If you suddenly shiver for no apparent reason it is said that somebody is walking over your grave — that is the piece of land where you will one day be buried.

In the 1790's William Doggett committed suicide in Dorset. His ghost now haunts Eastbury House and a headless coachman has been seen to stop and pick him up. In 1845 Doggett's coffin was opened to reveal his rosy-faced corpse which had no signs of decay, causing the local people to think that he was a vampire.

The skull of General Louis Joseph de Montcalm, who died in battle in 1759, is preserved in a glass case at the Chapel of Ursuline nuns.

Epitaph:
Here lies a man who met his fate
Because he put on too much weight.
To overeating he was prone
But now he's gained his final STONE.

Early medieval witches were thought to have the power to suck blood from sleeping men.

Hurstmonceaux Castle in East Sussex is haunted by a giant phantom drummer who beats his drum along the battlements of the castle.

A hell hound known as **Hearne the Hunter** is a famous monster who is said to tear through the grounds of Windsor Great Park, followed by a pack of phantom hounds.

A fully grown human brain weighs three pounds.

What musical instrument does a skeleton play?

A trom-bone.

The body of a Bronze Age woman, presumably a sorceress, was discovered buried with the claw joint of a lynx, the bones of a weasel, spines of snakes, horses' teeth, rowan twigs and a broken knife, all believed to possess magical powers.

On 15 September, 1651, a bearded female was put on display. She was only twenty years old and yet possessed a thick bushy beard, better than any man could grow.

A biological freak called the **Spider Monster** appeared in an American horror film in 1958. This gigantic eight-legged monster spun a web like a huge net which caught human beings, which the monster devoured.

In Somerset is a stone called the **Caractacus Stone**. Nobody knows its origin, but treasure is supposed to be buried underneath. The stone is haunted by the ghost of a man who tried to dig up the treasure and was crushed by the stone.

The road between Knockandhu and Milton of Auchriachan in Scotland is haunted by the **Phantom Hound**, whose appearance always precedes disaster. The hound is said to leave tracks in the snow as large as a man's hand.

To make yourself look like a Mummy, wet some thick paper towels. Wring out the water until they are almost dry, then lay them across your face so that they look like wrinkled bandages. Don't forget to leave spaces for your eyes and nose so that you can see and breath. Wear some old white pyjamas, white gloves, plimsolls and a white scarf around your neck and you will look like the Mummy from the Tomb.

Charlotte, having seen his body,
Borne before her on a shutter,
Like a well-conducted person
Went on cutting bread and butter.

Barbeck House in Argyll is haunted by the ghost of a girl with long hair and a shawl over her head, who disappears if anyone approaches her.

How did the dentist become a brain surgeon?

His drill slipped.

Hazel and apple trees were so sacred in Ireland that to chop one down was punishable by death.

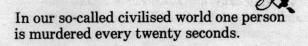

In our so-called civilised world one person is murdered every twenty seconds.

97

A particularly unpleasant ghost haunts the beach at Staithes, North Yorkshire. Whilst on the beach in 1800 the head of **Hannah Grundy** was sliced off by a falling rock. Her grisly ghost now wanders amongst the sunbathers.

Here's your chance to join the **Count Dracula Fan Club** — just send your name, address, and blood sample to. . . .

In the Middle Ages during a time of sickness it was believed that a monster bird called **Caladrius** sat at the end of the sick person's bed. If it looked towards the person who was ill, he would recover; if the monster looked away, there was no hope. . . .

The Elizabethan philosopher Francis Bacon died from a chill which he caught when he was trying to freeze a chicken by stuffing it with snow.

The Chief Magistrate's Palace in Florence is decorated with portraits of hanged men, painted by the famous artist, Botticelli.

The Chinese believed that a piece of jade prevented the decay of a corpse. Prince Liu Sheng and his wife in the second century BC were buried in suits made out of over 2000 squares of jade.

NEWSFLASH:
Last night a man fell into a barrel of beer and came to a bitter end.

Underneath a humble stone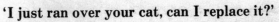
Sleeps a skull of one unknown.
Deep in Eden's bed was found,
Was the luckless owner drowned?
What matter, since we all must die,
Whether death be wet or dry?

'I just ran over your cat, can I replace it?'
'Depends how good you are at catching mice.'

Why did Dr. Skull's patients keep dying?
Because he was always sticking the knife in.

The first deaths during the American Civil War did not occur on the battlefield, but by demonstrators against the war throwing stones.

Death is a fisherman; the world we see
A fish-pond is, and we the fishes be;
He sometimes angles, like doth with us play,
And slyly take us one by one away.

Borthwick Castle in Scotland is haunted by a ghost who looks like a young boy, but is actually Mary, Queen of Scots, who escaped from the castle disguised as a page.

Among the many human horrors that the nineteenth century American showman P.T. Barnum put on display was Millie-Christine, the 'two-headed' girl.

Which airlines do ghosts use?

British Scareways.

While Mrs. Euphemia Johnson was drinking her afternoon tea she spontaneously burst into flames and died. Her body burned so quickly that her charred remains were found inside her unburnt clothes.

NEWSFLASH:
Count Dracula has denied that he is to marry Viscountess Vampire. They remain just good fiends.

Today half the total of dead in Great Britain are cremated rather than buried. Which means there will be fewer skeletons lurking around in the future!

A monster dog with three heads and a serpent's tail was thought by the Greeks to guard the entrance of Hades — the home of the dead — and prevented anyone from leaving.

'Excuse me, but your wife just fell in that well.'
'That's OK, nobody drinks water from there anymore.'

The manor house at Sandford, Orcas, Dorset, is haunted by no fewer than fourteen ghosts, including a white smocked farmer who hanged himself there in 1700, and a mad footman.

What does Dracula have at 10.30 every morning?

A coffin break.

 Madam Tussaud's in London receive at least two letters a week from people who want to sleep in the Chamber of Horrors!

 At 25 Montague Road, Cambridge, the ghost of a woman in a hammock appeared to a little boy in the garden. He later found out that an aunt of his had died on this spot before he was born.

 In the Middle Ages in one short period over thirty thousand cases of werewolfery were reported in France alone.

 Using a red lipstick draw two puncture marks on your neck and a thin trickle of blood to make it look as if you have been bitten by a vampire.

 Two-headed monsters are scary enough, but a fire-breathing monster called **Ghidrah** was created by Japanese film makers and had no less than three heads! To make matters worse, this horror cannot be destroyed by any weapon.

Viking witches raised evil spirits to haunt an enemy by placing a horse's head with its mouth open on a pole outside the enemy's house.

The first blood transfusions used animal's blood. The patients frequently died as a result.

In 1512 a creature was born which became known as the **Monster of Ravenna**. It had a human body with a horn on its head, two wings, only one foot which had claws, and an eye in its one knee-cap.

Why was Count Dracula happy to help young vampires?

Because he liked to see new blood in the business.

To work revenge on an enemy, witches made a figure of their victim out of wax, dough or lime and plunged them in boiling water.

Last night I slew my wife,
Stretched her on the parquet flooring;
I was loth to take her life,
But I had to stop her snoring.

Dwarf-like creatures with strange pointed skulls have been born. They are known as pin-heads and were once a great attraction at side shows.

In Germany it is a custom to place a coin in the mouth of a corpse, otherwise it is believed he will turn into a vampire.

Why did they put a wall around the graveyard?

Because people were dying to get in.

At Crathes Castle, Aberdeenshire, Scotland, the ghost of a **Green Lady** is seen walking across a room and lifts a baby out of the fireplace. During alterations to the castle the bodies of a woman and a child were discovered under the floorboards.

To turn yourself into an ogre, get some old bones from the butcher (tell him that they are for your dog). Paint some red 'blood' onto the bones, and push them down your sleeves when wearing an old jacket and let the bones protrude through any holes.

A fun game for parties is that of **Zombies**.
To play the game one person is chosen to
be a Detective, another a Sorcerer, and
the rest of the players are Zombies. The
Detective is sent out of the room, and
whilst he is away the Sorcerer is chosen.
When the Detective comes back into the
room, the Sorcerer will make all sorts of
motions. He may lift up one leg, raise an
arm, or clench a fist. The Zombies will do
exactly the same. The secret is for the
sorcerer and the Zombies to all move at
exactly the same time for the object of
the game is for the Detective to guess
who the Sorcerer is.

One of the most famous ghosts in the
country is that of Lady Hilda who haunts
Whitby Abbey in Yorkshire. On summer
evenings Lady Hilda appears at one of
the windows at the north side of the
abbey, wrapped in a shroud.

Romans did not have their hair cut as we
do — they had it singed!

What did the polite vampire say to his
dentist after being treated?

'Fangs very much.'

On the night of the first new moon every
year, the ghost of a monk in a black habit
visits the ruined Guisborough Priory in
Yorkshire.

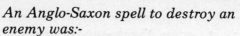

An Anglo-Saxon spell to destroy an enemy was:-
May you be consumed as coal upon the hearth,
May you shrink as mud upon a wall,
And may you dry up as water in a pail.
May you become as small as a linseed grain,
And much smaller than the hipbone of an itchmite,
And may you become so small that you are NOTHING.

During the reign of Charles I, dwarf Jeffery Hudson was presented to Queen Henrietta Maria baked in a pie.

To make monster hands, take some rubber gloves. Make sure that they are old ones which nobody will want anymore. Begin by sticking dried peas, beans or lentils all over them. Use the kind of glue which will not melt rubber. Now cut out some claws from a piece of card or from an old plastic detergent bottle, and glue those to the ends of the fingers. Finally spray the gloves green all over.

During the dissection of a toad almost 400 ants were found in its stomach.

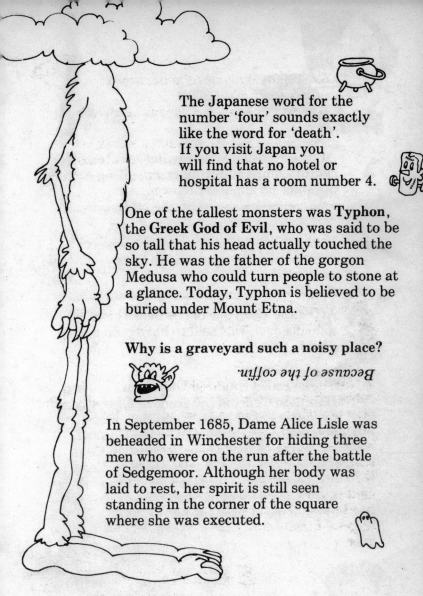

The Japanese word for the number 'four' sounds exactly like the word for 'death'. If you visit Japan you will find that no hotel or hospital has a room number 4.

One of the tallest monsters was **Typhon**, the **Greek God of Evil**, who was said to be so tall that his head actually touched the sky. He was the father of the gorgon Medusa who could turn people to stone at a glance. Today, Typhon is believed to be buried under Mount Etna.

Why is a graveyard such a noisy place?

Because of the coffin.

In September 1685, Dame Alice Lisle was beheaded in Winchester for hiding three men who were on the run after the battle of Sedgemoor. Although her body was laid to rest, her spirit is still seen standing in the corner of the square where she was executed.

 At a convent in Germany in the fifteenth century, nuns suddenly began biting each other for no apparent reason.

In the thirteenth century witches were accused of causing people to have nightmares

 Attila the Hun, one of the bloodthirstiest humans ever, was said to have been a dwarf.

The so-called **Haunted Gallery** at Hampton Court is the scene of a ghostly re-enactment of history. In 1542, just before her execution, Catherine Howard ran to the chapel where her husband was praying and banged on the door to plead for mercy. The guards dragged her away screaming. Her ghost still repeats this act in the hope of forgiveness.

 *Even a man who is pure in heart,*
And says his prayers by night,
May become a wolf when the wolfsbane blooms
And the Autumn moon is bright.

An horrific fire-spitting monster called the **Chimera** had the head of a lion, the body of a goat and a dragon's tail. It lived in Asia Minor and killed anyone who attempted to attack it.

A common test of witchcraft was to throw the suspected witch into some deep water. If the water rejected her and she floated then she was a witch. If she sank she was innocent.

Lady Frederick Campbell of Coombe Bank, Kent, was burnt to death in a fire in 1807. From her ashes the only piece of her that remained was one thumb, and her ghost has been searching for the missing piece ever since.

Veronica Shant, known as the '**gommin geek**', loved to bite off and swallow the heads of live chickens.

Carrie Akers in the nineteenth century became known as 'Quarrelsome Carrie' because of her very bad temper. She was nevertheless a popular attraction because not only was she a Dwarf, but also a Fat Lady and a Bearded Lady to boot.

Prime Minister, Benjamin Disraeli, slept with the legs of his bed in bowls of salt water to ward off evil spirits.

How can you tell if someone has a glass eye?

If it comes out in conversation.

To test the guilt or innocence of a witch, she was placed on one side of a scale, with a Bible on the other. If the witch was lighter than the Bible she was guilty.

O'er the rugged mountain's brow
Clara threw the twins she nursed,
And remarked, 'I wonder now
Which will reach the bottom first?'

A famous Scottish monster, other than the Loch Ness Monster, is the **Boobrie**. It resembles a massive duck, whose dreadful honk puts fear into anyone who hears it. It feeds off sheep and cows which it can devour in one mouthful.

Jeremy Bentham was an eighteenth century eccentric whose mummified body, dressed in his own clothes, can be seen preserved in a glass case at University College, London. His ghost haunts the college, wearing the same clothes as his body.

Epitaph:
Here lies Bill Dodge
Who dodged all good
And did a deal of evil
But after dodging all he could
He could not dodge the Devil.

110

To scare your friends at a party, tell them that you have a monster's head in a box. Say it is too horrible to look at, but they can feel it. On the table you have a box, with a hole inside just big enough to get a hand inside. The box is taped up so that it can never be opened, and inside is a melon with part of the top scooped out and filled with cold spaghetti. Push in a carrot to make a nose, some soft grapes can be stuck on with the help of a cocktail stick to be the eyes, and if you cut a slit for the mouth you can push in some macaroni teeth. This is what your friends will feel when they put their hand in the box. Ugh!

Where do mummies go swimming?

In the Dead Sea.

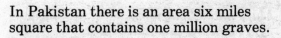

In Pakistan there is an area six miles square that contains one million graves.

In the fifteenth century witches were frequently tortured to make them confess their evil doings. Frequently they were hoisted into the air with weights attached to their bodies to pull their shoulders out of their sockets, leaving no visible marks of rough treatment.

The actor Bela Lugosi was the most famous screen Count Dracula and had such a sinister face that he needed to wear very little make-up. When he died in 1956, he was buried in the black cape with a red satin lining which he had worn so many times as the evil vampire.

Since the mid-fifteenth century, Triermain Castle in Northumberland has been haunted by a thin, shivering six-year-old child who sobs: *'cold for ever more.'* He died when his wicked uncle locked him outside in a snowstorm.

One of the most gruesome of all monsters is **Grendel**, a horrible beast who appears in an Old English poem called '**Beowulf**'. Grendel is killed by the hero of the poem, who later tries to cut off the monster's head as a trophy and it takes four men to carry it.

Mary had a little lamb,
You've heard this tale before,
But did you know she passed her plate
And had a little more?

To take a photograph of a King Kong monster, photograph a toy or model ape against a pale background. Without winding the film on, take a picture of some buildings from a distance. When the picture is developed you will see King Kong climbing over the buildings and looking 20 metres high.

What is a sick joke?

In 1539, during the reign of Henry VIII, it was possible for a man in London to be hanged for eating meat on a Friday.

In Norwegian folklore there are some nasty little creatures called the **Huldrefolk**, who are like little gnomes or trolls with a cow's tail. They snatch babies from their cradles and hide them under mountains.

Life is but a shade;
Man is but dust.
The clock dial says
Di-all we must.

'Twas as she tripped from cask to cask
That down a rabbit hole she fell.
Suffocation was her task,
She hadn't time to say farewell.

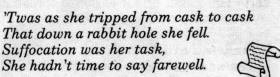

The ghost of old Tom Busby haunts Sandhutton in North Yorkshire where he was hanged for murder in 1702. His head lolls forward and the hangman's noose is still knotted around his throat. The landlord of Busby Stoop Inn always keeps a chair for the ghost who also haunts the pub.

113

What was Yorrick's nickname at school?

Numbskull

In one single year twenty-two lions killed 1,500 Kenyans.

A lion, once it has tasted human flesh becomes a man-eater for life.

 Gargoyles are grotesque stone heads that can be seen on medieval churches. To make your own, break up lots of old cardboard egg-boxes and mix them into a pulp by leaving them to soak in a bucket of water overnight. Next morning squeeze as much water as you can out of the pulp and then add some made-up wallpaper paste to it (about a third as much paste as there is pulp). Use this pulp to model a face. You might find it easier to spread it over a small cardboard carton or yoghurt pot as a base. Model a really ugly face and allow it to dry. To give it a stone appearance when dry, cover the whole face with glue and dip it into a bucket full of sand.

'Daddy, daddy, I don't want to go to Australia.'

'Shut up and keep digging.'

114

The horrible giant squid continues to grow throughout its entire life, whereas most animals reach adulthood and stop. By the end of its life it can be as much as fifty feet long.

Toads and frogs eat with their eyes! When they eat they close their eyelids and press their eyeballs down, which crushes the food down into their stomachs.

Renowned horror star Vincent Price acted in a real horror of a film in 1958 called **The Fly**. Through an experiment that went wrong Vincent Price as the scientist ended up with a fly's head instead of his own. His wife then decides to crush the head in a hydraulic press. . . . ouch!

'Mummy, mummy, daddy's going out!'

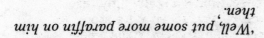

'Well, put some more paraffin on him then.'

There was a young lady from Gloucester
Whose parents thought they had lost her.
From the fridge came a sound
And at last she was found,
But the problem was how to defrost her!

'Doctor Skull, what is the best way for me to lose weight?'

'Get lock-jaw.'

From time to time there is a spectral flashback in time at St. Dunstan's Church in East Acton, London, when a procession of ghostly monks can be seen walking towards the chapel to sing mass.

A sideshow in Ancient Greece was to take a goat and cause it to go to sleep. This trick was done by pressing a certain spot on the goat's neck which stopped blood going through a certain artery leading to the brain.

How do you keep flies out of the kitchen?

Stand a bucket of manure in the dining room.

George Washington died on the last hour of the last day of the last week of the last month of the last year of the eighteenth century.

 What did the werewolf write on his Christmas cards?

Best vicious of the season.

750 years ago Brother Ignatius in the monastry at Elm in Cambridgeshire used to toll the bell if there was any danger of flooding. On one occasion he failed to do so and the village was flooded. Today his ghostly bell can be heard tolling if there is a death in the village.

70% of house dust consists of shed human skin. The adult human body sheds 50,000 microscopic flakes of skin every minute.

A Vampire, Countess Bathory, was found guilty of murdering over 600 young women and was executed in 1614 by being walled up alive.

How can you tell a monster from an elephant?

A monster never remembers.

Crabtree Hall, in the Yorkshire village of Cleghorn St. Percy, is haunted by two ghosts, a headless butler and a white lady. On winter evenings the butler can be seen standing in the corner of the dining room, and on occasions has opened the door to startled visitors. The white lady, a former occupant of the hall, glides slowly through the corridors before disappearing through a wall.

If you ever visit the Scottish lowlands, beware of the **NUCKELAVEE**, a monster that looks like a skinless old man with an enormous ugly head, no legs and very long arms that are just waiting to grab hold of you. His obnoxious breath kills any plant that he breathes on.

A sixty-eight-year-old Polish man was so frightened of vampires that he choked to death on a piece of garlic that he kept in his mouth to ward them off.

Ghosts can appear in various shapes and sizes and are not always human, they can be buildings too. In the 1920's two girls went on holiday to a village near Bury St. Edmunds and admired a very large house that they could see through wrought iron gates. They wondered who lived there. Returning a little while later they were amazed to see that where the house had been was a wilderness of weeds and trees. On asking about the house, nobody in the village could remember a time when a house had been on that spot.

Why are ghosts invisible?

Because they wear see-through clothes.

What game does Dr. Jeckyll enjoy playing?

Hyde and seek.

At the time of Elizabeth I, Lady Elizabeth Hoby beat her young son to death because he was slow and untidy with his schoolwork. Her old home of Bisham Abbey, Buckinghamshire, is haunted by a sobbing ghost who is seen gliding with a basin of water in front of her, in which she is trying to wash blood from her hands.

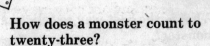

A chief of the Omaha Indian tribe, Blackbird, was buried sitting on his favourite horse.

How does a monster count to twenty-three?

On his fingers.

The Devil has appeared in more films than Jesus Christ.

A Tasmanian marsupial is known locally as the **'wolf'**. It eats other animals, but prefers to eat only the liver and naval passages, and any blood filled organs, and leaves the rest of the body for other predators called Tasmanian **'devils'**.

When Dracula telephones the undertakers, what is the first question he asks?

'Do you deliver?'

When a heron sits on the pinnacle of the cathedral spire at Chichester it is said to fortell the death of the Bishop.

When in 1944 United States Air Force men moved a stone from a witch's grave at Great Leigh in Essex, hens stopped laying, the milk of cows dried up, and the church bell tolled on its own. Things returned to normal when the stone was replaced.

What is the best way to talk to a monster?

By long distance telephone.

Since AD47 a Roman chariot pulled by a pair of screaming horses careers off the road and plunges into the moat at Black Greve Farm, just south of Birmingham. This occurs every Christmas Eve.

Alfred Hitchcock, director of the greatest horror movies, was born on Friday 13th.

Why do monsters forget everything you tell them?

Because it goes in one ear and out the others.

Why couldn't the skeleton fight back?

Because it had no guts.

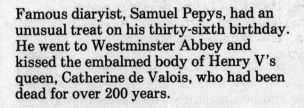

Famous diaryist, Samuel Pepys, had an unusual treat on his thirty-sixth birthday. He went to Westminster Abbey and kissed the embalmed body of Henry V's queen, Catherine de Valois, who had been dead for over 200 years.

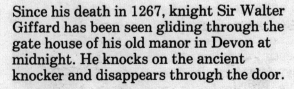

Since his death in 1267, knight Sir Walter Giffard has been seen gliding through the gate house of his old manor in Devon at midnight. He knocks on the ancient knocker and disappears through the door.

Where do ghosts study?

At ghoulage.

In 1906 there was an horrific disaster in northern France when a coal mine collapsed and more than 1000 men were killed. A few miners survived and when they were eventually brought to the surface they thought they had been trapped for four or five days — they had been in the mine for three weeks!

Epitaph of John Miles:

 This tombstone is a Milestone,
Ha! How so?
Because beneath lies Miles,
Who is now Miles below.

Who looks after ghosts in a phantom football team?

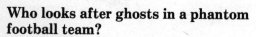
The ghoul keeper.

Count Dracula did actually exist, believe it or not. His name was Prince Vlad Dracula and became known as '**Vlad the Impaler**' because he used to stick his victims on to wooden stakes so that they died a slow agonising death. He then cooked their bodies and fed them to their unsuspecting families. After battles he held huge massacres and once burned 300 men alive. Fortunately he was beheaded, so is not around to terrorise us anymore.

What is the best way to describe horror films?

Spooktacular.

Witchcraft was at its height between 1560 and 1660 and all storms, plagues, famines and disasters were blamed on to witches.

When Mohammed Ali was ruler of Egypt he had two complete armies of one-eyed men.

Where do ghouls swim?

On the South Ghost.

Kate Oatway was starved to death and walled up in a room at Chambercombe Manor in Devon. Her grisly body was not discovered for over 150 years, when in 1865 an unfortunate farmer pulled back the rotting curtains of a four-poster bed to reveal Kate's skeleton. Nobody knows why she was allowed to die, but her ghost still wanders down the corridors of the manor.

The ugliest woman in the world is said to have been Julia Pastrana, who had flesh like raw meat, a huge distorted chin so that her mouth would hardly open, jagged teeth, a big crooked nose and deep piercing eyes.

 In a 1962 film a monster called **Reptilicus** was dug up in Denmark. It was a pre-historic lizard, but once in a laboratory it comes alive again and starts, like so many monsters, to destroy everything in sight.

 To turn yourself into a ghost, get someone to take a picture of you standing on a staircase, or in a room. As soon as the picture is taken, you quickly move out of the way and **without moving the position of the camera at all**, get the photographer to take another picture without winding the film on. When the picture is developed there will be a picture of you, but like a ghost you will be able to see right through you.

 When making eerie sounds and noises, especially when tape-recording them, use your bathroom as a studio. Everything will echo eerily.

The horse bit his master;
How came this to pass?
He heard the good Pastor
Say, 'All flesh is grass!'

For over 100 years climbers on the Beglic Glacier in Western Canada have seen the body of a man perfectly preserved in the slow-moving ice.

What runs around Paris in a plastic bag at lunch-time?

The lunch-pack of Notre Dame.

On Good Friday 1264, Lady Blanche de Warenne was accidentally killed during a battle at Rochester Castle in Kent. On the anniversary of her death her ghost with an arrow through its heart wanders through the castle.

Legend has it that if you walk around the preaching cross in the graveyard at Weobley in Herefordshire you can conjure up the Devil. Not many people dare try it!

*Little Jimmy Rose
Sat on a pin.
Little Jimmy rose.*

What is the name of Dracula's favourite cook?

Fangy Craddock.

 Since 1840 every U.S. president elected in a year ending with a zero has died in office.

In a 1963 American horror film called **The Slime People**, horrible prehistoric blobs of slime attempt to control the world.

All over Lincolnshire the legend of the **Black Dog** is known. A very rich widow was murdered for her money many years ago, and the site where her house once stood is now haunted by a Phantom Hound with a woman's face.

At Cadbury Camp in Somerset many pagan rituals, including Black Magic, are known to have taken place on May Day and Midsummer's Eve.

What should you do if you find a werewolf sleeping in your bed?

Sleep somewhere else.

During a thunderstorm in France in 1968, lightning struck a flock of sheep killing all the black ones and leaving the white ones untouched.

Why did the monster go to hospital?

To have his ghoul stones removed.

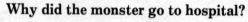

A modern monster called **HAL 9000**
appeared in the film **2001: Space Odyssey**.
Hal 9000 is a computer that becomes
power mad and attempts to kill the
astronauts. To put an end to him, the
computer is taken to pieces.

The living are outnumbered by the dead
thirty to one.

In the sixteenth century if children died
during childbirth, the midwife was
accused of being a witch and was thought
to have crushed the child's brain or
sucked out all its blood. In 1587 midwife
Walpurga Hausmannin was tried on
forty-three charges and was burnt at the
stake.

Grace Daniels, a rival for the ugliest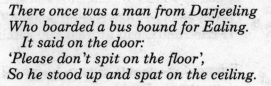
woman in the world title, was known by
many as the '**mule woman**' although it is
said that her face bore a greater
resemblance to a hippopotamus.

There once was a man from Darjeeling
Who boarded a bus bound for Ealing.
  It said on the door:
'Please don't spit on the floor',
So he stood up and spat on the ceiling.

Some insects can live as long as a year
after their heads have been chopped off!
They respond to light and heat still, even
though they can't see where they are
going.

The ghost of Lady Margaret de Pomeroy haunts her former home at Berry Pomeroy Castle in Devon. Lady Margaret and her sister, Lady Eleanor both fell in love with the same man. Lady Margaret was locked in a dungeon by her sister and left to die. Her ghost now walks the castle ramparts, beckoning people to their death.

To make fake fingernails, cut them out of an old plastic detergent bottle and paint them the colour you want. To attach them to your fingers, paint your nails with clear nail varnish and carefully place the fake nails on your real ones. Allow the polish to dry and the nails will stick.

 If you visit Trinity College, Cambridge, you will see in New Court a ghost hunting kit with which ghosts can be tracked down.

 From 1623 to 1633 Bishop Johann Georg II tried and burnt at least 600 witches.

 What walks backwards through a wall going 'er . . . Boo'?

A nervous ghost.

It was once the law that if a man survived three attempts to hang him he was set free.

Emily Kaye was chopped up and burned by the man she loved in 1924. Today her ghost, dressed in a long white gown, haunts Pevensey, Sussex, and walks along the shore near the coastguard's house where she was murdered.

One of the most horrible creatures imaginable is a large eye that crawls along the ground on its own, propelled by tentacles, and lets out a poisonous gas. It was the 'star' of a horror film called, believe it or not, **The Crawling Eye**.

To give yourself a horrible looking scar, make a special gelatine mixture. Put one teaspoon of gelatine powder into a cup, add one drop of red food colouring and one teaspoonful of hot water. Mix very quickly with a spoon, or an old lolly stick. As soon as the mixture is cool, stick the mixture to your cheek and push it around to make a lumpy uneven surface. This will stick on any part of your body and will look like a nasty burn. To remove it, simply peel it off.

The last European witch was burned in Switzerland in 1782.

The 1933 King Kong was a hand puppet 15.24 cms (6 ins) high.

Twenty-five years after the death of Dean Liddell, the father of the real Alice in Wonderland, his profile appeared in damp stains on the walls of his cathedral, Christ Church in Oxford, and remained there perfectly recognisable for three years.

MURDERER: *What are my chances of going to heaven?*
PRIEST: *Let's just say, if I was you I'd wear shorts to the funeral.*

The most important tool of a witch is the **ATHAME** — a black-handled, double-edged dagger used to cast magic spells and invoke spirits.

Japanese ghosts are always shown in pictures to have no legs.

In New York in 1964 a surgeon was about to perform a post-mortem on a corpse when it leapt up and grabbed him by the throat. The surgeon died of shock.

In 1954 a horror film created a creature that was a cross between a man and a frog. This horrifyingly ugly monster was called the **Creature from the Black Lagoon**, because it lived in the Amazon jungle deep in the mud.

A fun game to play at parties or even quietly on a rainy day is **'Create a Monster'**. Write on a number of pieces of card the names of a number of monsters, and get each player to pick a card. Without showing the card to any other person, each player must begin to draw his monster — it might be how he or she imagines the Creature from the Black Lagoon, or Godzilla, to look. When the drawing is complete, each player holds his picture up and the others have to guess the name of each monster.

'There's been an accident,' they said,
'Your husband's cut in half; he's dead!'
'Indeed!' said Mrs. Brown, 'Well, if you please,
Just give me the half that's got my keys.'

 What do you call something with three eyes, two mouths and four noses?

Extremely ugly!

Susan and Deborah, aged five and three, weighed 205 pounds and 124 pounds respectively.

The ghost of a lady who wrings her hands in desperation is said to appear every night at Thurstaston Hall in Cheshire.

Some babies of the Chinook tribe in India are strapped between two boards until they are one year old to give them a flat skull.

What happened to the boy who slept with his head under the pillow?

The fairies took all his teeth away.

DOCTOR FRANKENSTEIN: *Tell me, Igor, where is the monster?*
IGOR: *He just went to town to post 26 Father's Day cards.*

Up until 1971 the act of setting fire to a ship was punishable by death.

The famous witches' black cat was thought to be a demon that had taken on an animal shape.

The famous author Tolkein once wrote a book called **The Adventures of Tom Bombadil**, and in it he described a horrible slimey monster called 'The Mewlip' who reaches out of the slime and drags your body back into it.

The shadows where the Mewlips dwell
Are dark and wet as ink,
And slow and softly rings their bell,
As in the slime you sink. . . .

A bedroom at the Royal Oak public house
in Chichester is haunted by a mysterious
lady who glides across the room and
disappears into a full-length mirror.

At the beginning of this century a woman
called Betty Lou Williams had four legs
and three arms.

The slopes of Ben Buie in Argyll,
Scotland, are haunted by the ghost of
Euan, who in life had his head chopped
off in an attack. His horse returned home
with his headless body.

Give yourself a horror appearance by
putting a rolled-up towel around your
shoulders before getting dressed. This
will give you a hunchback. To add to the
effect, place a small pebble in one of your
shoes to give yourself a limp.

To create a ghostly tapping sound, tie a
button onto a piece of cotton and hang it
outside their bedroom window. When the
wind blows during the night there will be
a gentle tap, tap, tap, at the window.
They won't dare get up to see what it is!

Twenty thousand years ago men on a
hunt used to drink blood.

133

The most common names for the black cats of witches were:
Pyewacket, Tibb, Vinegar-Tom, and **Grizel**.

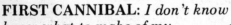

FIRST CANNIBAL: *I don't know know what to make of my husband these days.*
SECOND CANNIBAL: *How about a curry.*

William Coom of Leicester, was born in 1840 on a Thursday; was married on a Thursday; was never ill on any day other than a Thursday; and quite naturally died on a Thursday in 1890.

MOTHER MONSTER: *Don't sit in that chair, it's for Rigor Mortis to set in.*

Melbourne Hall in Derbyshire is said to be haunted by the ghost of a beautiful lady called Betty Coke. At the time of her death she was working on a tapestry and left it unfinished. It is said that she returns to the Hall from time to time to add a few more stitches.

William Durks was born with two heads fused together so that although he only had one mouth and one nose, he had three eyes.

134

To distort your features beyond recognition, use sticking plaster. Cut a strip of flesh coloured plaster about 5cm long. Put one end in position and stick it down. Now pull your skin into the position you want and stick the rest of the plaster down. Cover it up with make-up and you will look pretty gruesome. Don't keep it on too long though — you might stay like that!

Joan of Arc was burned at the stake when she was nineteen.

Little Willie, late one night,
Lit a stick of dynamite.
Don't you think he had a cheek?
It's been raining Willie for a week.

Bug-eyed monsters called Saucer Men appeared in a 1957 horror film called **Invasion of the Saucer People**. The creatures were destroyed, strangely enough, by bright lights which appeared to be just too much for them.

What is Dracula's nickname?

The pain in the neck.

The digestive juices of crocodiles contain so much hydrochloric acid that six inch nails swallowed by crocodiles have been dissolved.

Czar Peter III of Russia ruled for some six months until he was assassinated. He was crowned thirty-five years after his death, and his coffin was opened to do this.

How can you tell if a mummy is angry?

He flips his lid.

A punishment for witches was a **'witch's bridle'**. It was made of iron and forced four sharp prongs into the mouth. Two pressed against the tongue and the other two against the cheeks.

Richard Oastler, a nineteenth-century campaigner for factory reform, once told someone that if he didn't believe in ghosts he (Oastler) would return and haunt him after his death. He kept his promise and Oastler's ghost first made its presence felt on the very day of his death.

Two years after his funeral, the body of Oliver Cromwell was removed from its coffin and was publicly hanged and beheaded. The head was placed on a spike and displayed on the roof of the Houses of Parliament, where it remained for nearly 25 years.

A gigantic bird of prey called **Roc** appears in the ancient Arabian Knights tales, and although one Roc carries Sinbad the Sailor to safety in one story, a two-headed Roc almost kills him in another.

Did you hear about the Irish ghost?

It climbed over walls.

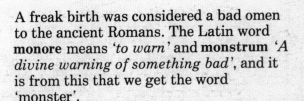

A couple of centuries ago a common practice was for people to swallow live frogs to clear out their systems.

A freak birth was considered a bad omen to the ancient Romans. The Latin word **monore** means '*to warn*' and **monstrum** '*A divine warning of something bad*', and it is from this that we get the word 'monster'.

In 1820 following a revolt, 176 prisoners were taken by the French and locked up. The following morning 173 of them were found to have committed suicide.

Many children have a horror of dentists, which is not surprising when you consider the fact that from the mouths of children in England and Wales dentists extract four tons of rotten teeth every year.

Silky was a famous Northumberland witch who lived in a river bank shack, and wore nothing but black. She had mysterious powers, such as being able to make horses bolt for no apparent reason, and at a bridge named Silky's Bridge strange things still happen and it has been the scene of many car accidents, even though Silky has been dead for some 200 years.

In 1878 the Queen of Madagascar was buried in a coffin of 30,000 silver coins riveted together, disproving the saying that you can't take your money with you when you die!

Most ghosts appear only at night, but not Lady Anne Streatfield. During her lifetime she had a passion for horses, and today in broad daylight her ghost can be seen riding side-saddle down the leafy lanes around Chiddingstone Castle, her former home, in Kent.

'Bicorn and Chichevache' were two monsters said by writers in the fifteenth century to live off the flesh of men and women who were good. The monsters were said to be extremely thin for this reason!

1st MONSTER: *That girl over there just rolled her eyes at me.*
2nd MONSTER: *Well roll them back again, she might need them.*

The Chinese considered strangulation a much less severe punishment than being beheaded, because the body was not permanently disfigured.

Determined to get it right, Queen Catherine Howard decided to rehearse her execution. On the day before she was beheaded she asked for the executioner's block to be brought to her cell so that she could practise.

To make a giant monster or abominable snowman, get some old cardboard boxes and stand four or five on top of each other. Push a pole through the top boxes to make the arms, and a paper bag stuffed with newspaper to make the head. Pad out the monster by sticking screwed up sheets of newspaper over the whole body except the face. When it is all dry, stick white tissues over the creature, starting at the top and working downwards until it is completely covered. Finally paint on a scary face and you have your own huge monster.

How does a ghost like his drink in hot weather?

Ice ghoul?

On the eve of Alexander the Great's expedition to Asia a statue of Orpheus is said to have sweated for several days.

Where do vampires think the happiest place to have a party is?

The morgue the merrier.

A fire which destroyed much of the town of Balingen in Germany was blamed on to a woman suspected of being a witch and she was publicly stoned in the street.

A young London secretary called Irene Munro was murdered and buried on the beach at Pevensey in Sussex by her murderer. Sometimes a green light can be seen hovering over the beach. It is thought to be the wraith of poor Irene.

Thousands of years BC stories were told of a fabulous dragon monster called 'Zu' who stole the laws of the universe which were inscribed on stone tablets. The monster was said to have been killed as a result.

The wife of Ulysses S. Grant, former President of the United States, was cross-eyed, but the President would not allow her to have an operation because he liked her that way.

Lightning kills more people in the USA than any other natural disaster. Almost 500 people die each year after being struck.

In 1783 Charles Byrne of Littlebridge, Ireland, died of tuberculosis. He was over seven feet tall. Surgeon, John Hunter, paid £500 for Byrne's body so that he could display it in his museum.

Where do ghosts go on holiday?

Goole (Ghoul).

To turn yourself into a cyclops, a one eyed monster, make yourself a large eye from half a table tennis ball. Make it look like a real eye by colouring it with felt-tip pens. Stick it to your forehead with fleshcoloured plasticine. Finally, take a bandage and loosely bandage your head so that only your cyclops eye sticks out, but so that you can breathe and see where you are going through the bandages.

141

Germ warfare reached its height in the fourteenth century when corpses infected with the **Black Plague** were catapulted at the enemy during a war in Genoa. Many of the country's inhabitants caught the disease and died.

 In 1890, 180,000 mummified cats were auctioned in Liverpool.

What do you call a skeleton in a kilt?

Boney Prince Charlie.

In 1579 at Chelmsford, Essex, Margery Stanton was charged with witchcraft when her neighbours suffered illness and death after a quarrel with her.

Ye Olde Gatehouse, Highgate, London, is haunted by Widow Marnes, who was murdered for her money along with her pet cat. Her black robed figure now haunts the Minstrel's Gallery if ever children or pets are around.

During the Middle Ages it was believed that anyone who was a werewolf, whilst in human form had the hair on the inside and turned their bodies inside out to become a werewolf.

'I used to be a werewolf, but I'm alright nooooooooooooowwwwww!'

 In 1789 the average life expectancy for males was thirty-four years five months and thirty-six years five months for females.

Charles VIII of France had six toes on one foot. He introduced a fashion for having shoes with a square tip so that nobody would notice his own foot.

To make yourself appear to have feet like Frankenstein's monster, get two small shoe boxes, both the same size. Paint them black so that they look like shoes, and sellotape the lid to the bottom of the box. Make a hole in the top of each box just large enough for you to get your foot through, and you will have huge square feet, just like the monster.

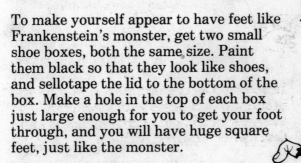

In Siberia it is so cold that gravediggers have to make a fire where they want the grave to be so that the ice will thaw.

 Baron Dominique Larry, Napoleon's surgeon, could amputate a man's leg in fourteen seconds.

What does a monster call his parents?

Dead and mummy.

143

Witches draw a magic circle around a person on which they are performing a magic spell to protect them from evil spirits.

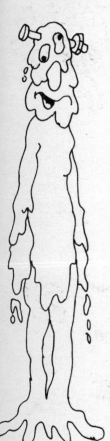

The Old Parsonage at Handforth, Cheshire, is haunted by the ghost of an old lady, frightened to death by a visit from Bonnie Prince Charlie in 1745.

Frankenstein's monster was called the 'Modern Prometheus'. Prometheus was a Greek figure, like Dr. Frankenstein, who created men out of mud and water.

The great musician Mozart was actually buried in an unmarked pauper's grave, and only one person walked alongside the coffin at the funeral.

Little Willie, in the best of sashes,
Played with fire and burned to ashes.
Very soon the room got chilly,
But no one liked to poke poor Willie.

Victoria Woodhull feared that she would die of old age if she went to bed, so she spent the last four years of her life sitting in a chair and died at the age of eighty-seven.

The Grey Lady of Bury St. Edmunds, who now haunts the ruined abbey, is thought to have been Maude Carew, a nun who poisoned the Duke of Gloucester in 1447.

To make a gorgon's head, use a melon as the head, decorate it with pieces of fruit to make a mouth, eyes and a nose. Cover lots and lots of pieces of wire with green tape or crepe paper, and bend them into the shape of curly snakes. Stick them into the melon to look like the gorgon's 'hair' of live snakes. Make her look as horrible as you possibly can.

What happened to the wolf that fell into the washing machine?

He became a wash and wear wolf.

The Battle Cannas in 216 BC covered an area roughly the size of Hyde Park. Over 76,000 Roman infantry were killed.

The ghost of orphan Mary Jay haunts her burial place at Widecombe in Devon. A phantom figure without legs has been seen stooping over her grave, and flowers are often left behind — but nobody knows who places them there.

American strong-man, Frank Richards could withstand a cannon-ball fired at his abdomen, a force of 47.17 kg (104 lbs).

There was an old lady from Ryde
Who ate some apples and died.
The apples fermented inside the lamented,
And made cider inside her inside.

At Seafield Bay in Suffolk the screams of witches can be heard at night, shrieks of agony as they were tortured by Witch Finder General, Matthew Hawkins.

What is the difference between a musician and a corpse?
One composes, the other decomposes.

The oldest brain matter yet unearthed is six-thousand years old — discovered by archaeologists in Florida.

Horror movie stars Peter Cushing, Vincent Price and Christopher Lee were all born on May 27th.

Killer bees have been responsible for the deaths of between 200—300 people in Brazil in the last twenty years.

On joining a coven, witches are injected with a dye between the upper and middle joints of the third finger of their right hand. This mark remains forever. The top joint represents hazel, the tree of healing, whilst the middle joint stands for the blackthorn, tree of cursing and death.

Porlock Hill in Somerset is haunted by ghostly grey horses, spectres of a run-away team killed on this hill.

Which monster was also President of France?

Charles de Ghoul.

A window cleaner falling to his death in Paris was heard to shout:
'I'm alright so far!' **as he passed a third-floor window.**

Hatto II of Germany found a solution to the 914 AD famine. He gathered all the poor people together in a barn, saying that he was going to feed them, then he locked them in and set fire to the barn!

What kind of horse does a headless horse-man ride?

A nightmare.

The monster blue whale, one of the biggest creatures in the world, can go a whole six months without eating. It has enough blubber on its body to survive.

A monster that need not cause you too much worry is the **Goofus**. It is a kind of bird that was discovered by lumberjacks and appears to be harmless. It flies backwards and builds its nest upside down.

Which ballet do monsters like best?

Swamp Lake.

What wears a black cape, flies around at night and sucks people's blood?

A mosquito wearing a black cape.

To turn yourself into a '**corpse**', cover your face with white make-up, or talcum powder so that your skin looks drained of blood. Draw a thin trickle of blood from the corner of your mouth with a red lipstick. Lie on the ground and practise keeping your eyes open without blinking.

148

At Crosby on the Isle of Man there is the legend of Buggane, a witch who could not bear the sound of the church bells and tore the roof off the church.

On 24th November 1779 a ghost appeared to Lord Lyttleton telling him that he would die within 3 days. He died on the 27th November. The moment Lord Lyttleton died his ghost was seen by a friend. Lyttleton's ghost said: *'It's over with me, Andrews.'* Andrews threw his slippers at him, believing it to be Lyttleton in person!

What is a stupid monster?

A dummy-mummy.

The most elusive monster of all is the **Loch Ness Monster**, which has a snake-like head and a body that some say is 12m (40ft) long, and is sighted numerous times each year. With a depth of 230m (750ft) scientists say that it is quite possible that a monster could live in Loch Ness.

The Lord saw good, I was lopping off wood,
And down fell from the tree.
I met with a check, and I broke my neck
And so death lopp'd off me!

Ghosts very rarely speak and if they do it is usually only a very few words. Nobody has yet held a conversation with a ghost.

A magic charm used for making someone fall in love with you is said to be that of secretly adding three drops of your blood to a bowl of soup that the person is going to drink.

What does a ghost give his wife for Christmas?

A girdle so that she can keep her ghoulish figure!

A ghost is actually made of nothing and as an insubstantial being must be perfectly harmless, but frightening nevertheless because they represent the unknown.

If you look into a mirror and a friend looks over your shoulder your friendship will end.

Many people think it is unlucky to walk under a ladder. This stems from a time before the gallows were invented when murderers were hung from the top-most rung of ladders. Their ghost was thought to remain underneath the ladder.

The first record of a murder trial is of one held in 1700 BC

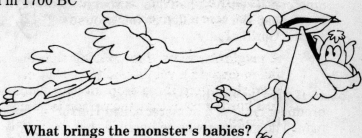

What brings the monster's babies?

The Frankenstork.

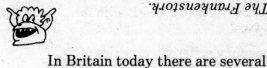

In Britain today there are several thousand active witches, and there are said to be over 10,000 in North America.

Dracula-like teeth can be cut out of a piece of shiny white card, and when placed under your top lip will look just like real fangs, especially if you decorate the ends of the fangs with non-toxic red felt-tip pen to look like dripping blood.

The human brain has no feeling at all. If someone were to cut into your brain you would feel nothing. The brain is, however, surrounded by a membrane that is filled with nerves which **can** feel pain.

At **Canewdon** in Essex the ghost of an old woman in a crinoline dress and poke-bonnet has been seen. She is thought to have been executed for witchcraft.

Frances Murphy, a bearded lady in the nineteenth century, had such a tough beard that she was billed at fair-grounds as the '**Gorilla Lady**.'

In Hollywood in the 1930s a film producer created a monster called Horror-man. The monster was so horrible that the film about him was never completed.

There are some fifty different varieties of sea snake, all of which have a bite that is ten times more dangerous than that of a cobra, which would mean death to anyone who has the misfortune of being bitten. Fortunately they do not live in the icy waters surrounding the British Isles.

One of the few ghosts to be photographed is the Brown Lady of Raynham Hall in Norfolk. She was pictured coming down the stairs in 1936. Her eye sockets are empty and she is said to herald a death.

Every witch writes down everything she learns in a large book which is called her **BOOK OF SHADOWS**. This book is destroyed on her death.

What did Frankenstein say when he was struck by lightning?

'Thanks, I needed that!'

In 1804 at Toulouse in France there was a shower of frogs during a storm. Roads and fields were full of the creatures.

Pant-y-Madog in Pembrokeshire, Wales is haunted by the **Hound of Death,** a spectral mastiff with blazing red eyes which runs from the castle to the town. Don't get in its way!

One horror sound which you can practice is laughing. It sounds surprising, but laughter can be made to sound very sinister indeed when you really try.

Peter the Great had his wife's lover executed and put his head in a jar of alcohol, which he made her keep beside her bed.

The convent of St. Edward in Shaftesbury is haunted by a very distressed monk. He hid some treasure somewhere in the Abbey, but died before he could tell anyone of the secret hiding place. Centuries later his ghost still tries to tell people where the treasure is. It is, as yet, unfound.

Turn your face into a human skull by painting it white with make-up. Put dark make-up around your eyes to make them look like sockets. Paint your nose black so that it looks as if it is missing, make it into a triangle if you can. Shade under your cheek bones, then finally across your mouth and covering your lips draw a series of black lines to look like a jaw with teeth. Scary! Finally drape a black shawl around your head so that just your face shows.

In the sixteenth century men were allowed to beat their wives before 10.00 pm.

Every night at Weare Giffard in Devon, Sir Walter Giffard sets out at midnight in search of his wife. He died in 1267 leaving behind his wife, and although she is now dead his ghost still carries on the search.

When someone becomes a witch they adopt two names — one is the coven name which they can use freely, the other is a secret name which they keep entirely to themselves. Part of the reason for this secrecy is magical.

Live toads have been found inside solid lumps of rock.

Why did the mummy leave his tomb after 3,000 years?

He felt he was old enough to leave home.

From Carlsbad Caverns in New Mexico each evening a quarter of a million bats fly out to find food.

One of the most popular television monsters to hit the small-screen is **The Incredible Hulk**, a giant green muscular creature with an amazing strength. The monster was created by accident when scientist Bruce Banner was exposed to a lethal dose of gamma rays which changed his chemical make-up. Now if he becomes angry he turns into the incredible hulk.

If you ever visit Fountains Abbey in Yorkshire, listen very carefully for the ghostly choir of monks which can often be heard chanting in the ruined Chapel of Nine Altars.

Incredible though it may sound for the twentieth century, one spooky object for which people are prepared to pay high prices is a human skeleton. In 1976 a skeleton cost around £80 to buy, but by 1978 the price had increased to nearly £250 and today a single skull can cost as much as £100. Who buys these gruesome bones? Not witches or monsters, but dental students and trainee doctors. We hope!

The **'Elephant Man'**, John Merrick, had a skull which was so large that it was impossible for him to sleep lying down because of the great weight. Instead he was forced to sleep sitting up with his hands clasped around his legs and his head resting upon his knees.

Lympne Castle, Kent, is haunted by the ghosts of six Saxons who were slaughtered during Norman times, and a Roman soldier who fell to his death from the castle ramparts.

Who won the monster's beauty contest?

No-one.

Early in 1948 **Life** magazine in America
printed a nine-page interview with the
Devil.

To make yourself two horns like the
Devil, cut out two semi-circles of card and
fold them into a pointed cone. Using a
couple of pieces of sellotape, stick the two
horns to your forehead, or push them out
through a couple of holes under your hat.
You little devil!

Which monster has the best hearing?

The eeriest.

The Globe Hotel in Ludlow, Shropshire, is
haunted by a soldier called Joe who died
there in 1513.

Women in the eighteenth-century often
had their gums pierced with hooks to
keep their false teeth in position!

In San Francisco, in 1962, an American
'witch' was arrested and accused of
charging 70 dollars to cure people's
illnesses with witchcraft. One of her cures
was for stomach pains, in which she rolled
an egg over the sufferer's stomach and
then smashed the egg on the floor.

The human kidney contains millions of little tubes, which if stretched out in a line would reach for about forty miles.

Why did Frankenstein's monster give up boxing?

He didn't want to spoil his looks.

Epitaph:

Here lies the body of Mary Anne Lowder
She burst whilst drinking a seidlitz powder.
Called from this world to her heavenly rest,
She should have waited till it effervesced.

How many vampires can fit into an empty coffin?

One — after that it isn't empty anymore.

Where does a vampire save his money?

 At a blood bank.

At Sandringham House in Norfolk a very weird phenomenon has been seen, described as a '**pulsating paper bag**' or a '**grotesque lung**'. Either way, it is very unpleasant.

A quiet game for a rainy day is to sit down with some friends and each draw the ugliest and most horrible monster that you can. The person who draws the most frightening is the winner.

Phantoms are more likely to haunt places that they visited during their lifetime than haunt the graveyards where they are buried.

St. John's College in Oxford is haunted by the ghost of Archbishop Laud who was behead in 1645. He is said to carry his head under his arm and bowl it along the library floor.

To make your own 'head', simply cover a balloon with papier maché and try and make it look like yourself. When it is dry, paint it a flesh colour so that it looks realistic. Now button your shirt or blouse up over your head so that you appear headless and carry your model under your arm. Like Archbishop Laud you can even bowl it along the ground.

Where does the Bride of Frankenstein have her hair done?

At the ugly parlour.

To make your voice sound ghostly, place a glass or jam jar over your mouth and speak into it. Your voice will echo and sound very different.

The muscles of an alligator's jaw are so strong that it can break off a person's arm just by closing its mouth.

Sixty thousand miles of blood vessels carry blood to every part of the adult body.

A hideous monster that you would not wish to meet is **Lamia**. She is half-woman and half-serpent and eats every child she can.

Simon Cunliffe, former squire of Wycoller Hall in Leicester, now haunts his former home on horse-back and his ghostly hunting horn can be heard when a tragedy is about to happen.

In late Renaissance Europe normal young children were fashioned into hunchbacks, and their bodies forced to grow distortedly purely so that they could be exhibited.

Many tales of phantom coaches were started by grave robbers in the nineteenth century. They transported the corpses in black coaches, first spreading frightening rumours so that nobody would be out at night to watch their illegal activities.

In Egyptian tombs the walls were coated with a poisonous substance that any would-be tomb robbers inhaled and died on the spot. The Egyptians were such masters of poisons that they retain their potency 3,000 years later.

What song did Count Dracula hate?

'Peg O' My Heart'.

A witch's fire is usually kindled **inside** the cauldron, not underneath it as is frequently shown in pictures.

A belief of the sixteenth and seventeenth centuries was that anyone who slept on feathers could not die peacefully. To overcome this, the dying person's pillow was removed to ease his passing.

However horrible or frightening something is, it is not true that a person's hair can turn white overnight.

A man's body contains 1.5 gallons of blood, and each cubic centimetre of blood contains 6.2 million red blood cells.

In his book **The Lord of the Rings**, Tolkein wrote about 'the Worms'. Not ordinary garden worms though, because these could fly and breathe fire like a dragon, and were extremely long and very spiteful creatures.

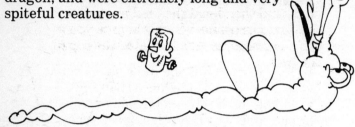

Tetcott in North Devon is haunted by a huntsman called John Arscott, a very weird man in life who took a bottle of flies to church to feed spiders and kept a tame toad called '**Old Dawty**'.

When the full moon is shining as clear as day,
John Arscott still hunteth the country, they say,
You may see him on Blackbird, and hear his full cry
The pack from Pencarrow to Dazzard go by.

The cry of a banshee is said to fortell a death.

During the 'witch-craze' of 1560-1660 more than 100,000 people were tortured and killed as witches.

To make a witch's hat, begin by cutting a circle of card about 30cm square. Draw a circle the size of your head in the centre of this circle and then one slightly smaller than your head. Cut out the smallest circle and then bend the card inwards on the next circle line, which will give you a tab all around on which to glue the top of the hat:

Next cut a circle 60cm in diametre. Make a cut from one edge to the centre and slide it around to form a cone. Glue this to the brim of your hat and it is finished.

Count Dracula was known in Rumania as **Voivode Vlad Teppish.**

Why didn't the skeleton want to go to school?

Because his heart wasn't in it.

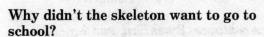

In Ancient Egypt baboons were believed to be companions of the god **Thoth** and were mummified and placed in tombs when they died.

If you ever visit the town of Chesterfield you will see that the church has a crooked spire. This is said to have been caused by the Devil resting upon it.

Mad Monica and Gruesome Gertie were walking down a road when Mad Monica pointed to a 50p piece in the road. Gruesome Gertie bent down in the road to pick up the 50p when a steam roller squashed her flat as a pancake. Mad Monica laughed and laughed. She knew all the time that it was only a 10p piece.

Avoid Burgh St. Peter's churchyard in Norfolk. It is haunted by a ghostly skeleton.

Why did the teacher always give the ghost bad marks?

Because he kept making a ghoul of himself.

The Chinese eat dogs, stewed, fried or minced.

 A famous double act was Tripp and Bowen. Tripp had no arms and Bowen no legs. They used to ride a tandem bicycle — Tripp would shout: *'Mind your step, Bowen!'* and Bowen replied: *'Keep your hands off me!'*

Epitaph of a doctor and grave robber:

Many I've raised from the grave
And pickled for dissection.
Saved in my turn I hope to have
A glorious resurrection.

At Thorp Arch, Yorkshire, the ghostly sound of phantom horses' hooves gallop across the cricket pitch, a flashback to the Battle of Bramham in 1408.

James Morris had an elastic skin, and could pull the skin of his chest up over his head.

What did one ghost say to another?

'I'm sorry, but I just don't believe in people.'

Twenty-six Popes have been murdered.

A strange Australian monster is the **BUNTIP**. It lurks in streams and swamps and feeds on human flesh. No living person can remember having seen one. If you get close enough to see it you are as good as dead.

Mac Norton, known as the human aquarium, swallowed three gallons of water and twenty-four live frogs in one go!

The most travelled corpse in the world is that of Eva Peron, better known as 'Evita'. Three years after her death in 1952 her body disappeared from Argentina and turned up in Milan. In 1971 it was dug up and buried in Madrid. On the death of Evita's husband in 1976 her body was finally taken back to Argentina where it now remains.

What did the werewolf eat after his teeth had been pulled?

The dentist.

Poor old Peggy's dead,
She died last night in bed.
We put her in a coffin
And she fell right through the bottom.

It was believed that when you sneezed an evil spirit would enter your open mouth. To prevent this happening, the person nearest you should say: *'Bless you!'*

Mrs. Lillian Browne was Matron at Thames Magistrates Court in London until her death in 1970. Since then her spectre has returned many times to keep an eye on proceedings.

166

To make a Hallowe'en lantern, get a large round turnip and cut a thick slice off the top. Scoop out the insides carefully, and cut out eyes, nose and teeth to make a face on one side of the turnip. Finally, place a candle or night-light inside the turnip and light it.

Who does a fiend enjoy seeing more than anyone else?

His ghoul fiend.

Over the years there have been many monsters in the TV series **Dr. Who**, but the favourites, and most feared, are the **Daleks** — mechanical monsters whose mission is to take over the universe. The Daleks are merely brains encased in an indestructable metal body with an electronic voice chamber, but have the power to exterminate anyone who gets in their way.

Which monster made friends with the three bears?

Ghouldilocks.

You readers all both old and young
Your time on earth will not be long
For death will come and die you must
And like all men return to dust.

167

Alfonso, the Ostrich Man, could chew up glass and pebbles, swallow nails and even soap, all washed down with petrol!

What did Count Dracula get after his first film?

Fang mail.

What do you call a ghost doctor?

A surgical spirit.

In 1951 a German carpenter was speared to death when an icicle pierced his heart.

One of the most dreaded monsters of the Middle Ages was the **Cokatrice**, sometimes called the **Basilisk**. Although it was only like a very tiny snake, about 15cm long, just one glance into its eyes meant immediate death.

Epitaph:

My wife is dead, and here she lies
Nobody laughs, nobody cries;
Where she has gone, or how she fares,
Nobody knows, and nobody cares.

If the present population of the earth were to continue to increase at its current rate, by the year 3530 AD the total weight of human flesh and blood would equal the weight of the earth.

The official portrait of the Duke of Monmouth was painted after his decapitation in 1685. This involved stitching the head back on the body so that it could pose for the artist.

If you were to completely skin a person the total weight of the skin alone would be six pounds.

What goes 'Ho, ho, ho, plop'?

Santa Claus laughing his head off.

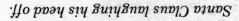

 The lanes around Market Bosworth, Leicestershire, are haunted by a phantom headless soldier.

Archduke Ferdinand of Austria was one of the vainest men that ever lived. So important was his appearance to him, he had himself sewn into his clothes so that they would fit perfectly. When he was shot in 1914 it was impossible to unbutton his uniform and so he bled to death inside.

Why are ghosts simple things?

Because you can see right through them.

 Witches classify each year in much the same way as the Chinese do. The years run in cycles of nine:

1982 — PLANT	1985 — SUN
1983 — ANIMAL	1986 — MOON
1984 — STONE	1987 — EARTH

1988 — FIRE
1989 — AIR
1990 — WATER

The people born in these years will have certain qualities, for example: if you were born in the Year of the Stone you will have sound logic and wise judgement. A man born in the Year of the Sun will be very strong, and a woman born in the Year of the Moon will be very beautiful and feminine.

The wicked Lady Howard of Okehampton Castle murdered three husbands and two children. As part of her penance her ghost rides nightly across Dartmoor in a coach made from the bones of her dead husbands.

In the nineteenth century, Jo-Jo the '**Dog-faced Boy**' toured the fairgrounds of Europe as a curiosity. His face was covered entirely with silky yellow hair.

What does a monster do when it rains?

Gets wet!

 Hickory Dickory Dock,
King Kong ran up the clock.
The clock is being repaired.

William Buckland, nineteenth century Dean of Westminster, ate Louis XIV's embalmed heart at dinner one evening.

Jack the Ripper was left-handed.

In the middle of the nineteenth century, one Lyddie Shears became known in Wiltshire as the 'Winterton Witch'. Her mysterious powers enabled her to tell poachers where hares could be found. One particular farmer melted down a silver sixpence and made it into a bullet, which he fired at a hare but he could not find the creature's body anywhere. Lyddie Shears was later found dead in her cottage. She had been killed by a silver bullet.

After the First World War a year-long flu
epidemic killed twenty million people —
more than were killed in the war.

Trojan helmets were adorned with
swastikas in the belief that they would
ward off the evil eye.

Mary had a little lamb,
Her father shot it dead.
And now it goes to school with her
Between two chunks of bread.

Notorious murderess, Mary Anne Cotton,
poisoned her four husbands and four
children, and was suspected of murdering
some fifteen other people, for which she
was executed by the hangman. Today her
ghost haunts the churchyard in West
Auckland, County Durham, where she is
buried.

Roaming the coast of Norway is
believed to be a giant monster
called **KRAKEN**; like a
monstrous squid it has tentacle-
like arms over 10m (35 feet) long
is bigger than a ship and
colours the water black so that it
can hide beneath the murky
surface.

1st NURSE: *How many patients has the new doctor had, is it three?*
2nd NURSE: *No, it's four. I attended all four funerals.*

The first man executed in an electric chair took eight minutes to die.

Runway 1 at London's Heathrow Airport is haunted by a bowler hatted gentleman, believed to be a businessman killed in an aircrash in 1948 when a DC3 aircraft burst into flames on take-off.

'Apple On The Mound' is an old Hallowe'en game that can be played by any number of people. A small apple or nut is placed on top of a large mound of flour in a dish. A spoon is laid on the table pointing inwards. Music should be played and stopped periodically (as with musical chairs) as the players walk around the table. When the music stops whoever is nearest the spoon must scoop away some of the flour without dislodging the apple. When the apply falls the unlucky person must get it out with their teeth, and if the apple has fallen in the middle they will get their face covered with flour.

Five enormous monsters stood under one umbrella, why didn't they get wet?

It wasn't raining!

Tarantula spiders do not eat their victims, but suck out the blood and body juices.

 In Norway and Scandinavian countries there are many legends about Trolls, ugly humpback dwarfs with long crooked noses. They are said to steal human babies and substitute them for their own, but you are safe if you stay in the sunshine. The sun's rays turn Trolls into stone.

 GIRL: *Do you believe in love at first sight?*
VAMPIRE: *No, love at first bite.*

 In Ancient Egypt **Anubis**, the god of the Dead, was believed to weigh the heart of the dead person in the underworld. If it did not balance with the feather of truth in the opposite scale it was eaten by **Ammit**, a horrible monster — half-lion, half-hippopotamus, with crocodile jaws.

 'Mummy, mummy, what's for dinner?'

'Shut up, and get back in the oven.'

174

In Brazil, if a man is suddenly seized with a sharp pain he not only calls in the doctor, but the witchdoctor too because he thinks he is bewitched and this produces a much sharper imaginary pain.

In Greek mythology monsters called the **Graiae**, who were horrible even in Hell, were said to protect the **Gorgons**. The Graiae were born grey in colour and only had one eye and one tooth between them, which they passed from one to another.

'I don't know what to make of my husband.'

'How about a hot-pot?'

An enormous giant called **Tityus** was feared by the Ancient Greeks. It was believed that when Tityus laid down he covered nine acres of ground.

Medea, a ferocious and jealous woman, wife of the Greek hero Jason, sought revenge when he fell in love with the King of Corinth's daughter. Medea sent her rival a very beautiful garment which was poisoned and burnt her to death as soon as she put it on.

175

The Rev. John Wesley, founder of
Methodism, experienced a poltergeist
haunting in his family home as a boy.

 Hungry man-eating birds with brass
beaks were thought to fly over Greece.
Known as the **Stymphalian** birds, they
had feathers like arrows which they could
shoot out and kill their victims with.

 At Lewisham in London mournful voices
are sometimes heard coming out of the
sky at 3.00am.

 According to a professional hangman a
person weighing 50.8 kg (8 stone) requires
a drop of 3.04 metres (10 feet), 0.6 metres
(2 feet) longer than that required for
someone weighing 88.9 kg (14 stone).

 **What do you call a monster with blocked
ears?**

Anything you like, he can't hear you.

The body of a hanged man found in a
marsh in 1950 was so well preserved that
the police were called in. The man had
been executed 1000 years earlier!

 **Did you hear about the cannibal who got
married and toasted his wife's parents at
the reception**

John Smith of Malton was executed on Christmas Eve 1705. After hanging by his neck for fifteen minutes he was cut down and found to be still alive.

How would a monster smell without a nose?

He'd still smell awful!

Down the street his funeral goes
As sobs and wails diminish.
He died from drinking varnish,
But he had a lovely finish.

I plant these shrubs upon your grave, dear wife,
That something on this spot may boast of life.
Shrubs must wither and all earth must rot;
Shrubs may revive: but you, thank Heaven, will not.

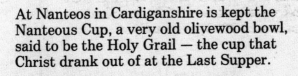

At Nanteos in Cardiganshire is kept the Nanteous Cup, a very old olivewood bowl, said to be the Holy Grail — the cup that Christ drank out of at the Last Supper.

The death penalty is still in force in Britain for anyone convicted of high treason.

A vampire who is equal only to Count Dracula himself is the horrible, bald-headed **NOSFERATU**. This phantom walks through the countryside at night and was the subject of the 1922 film **A Symphony of Terror**.

In 1869 a ten-foot tall, 3,000 pound petrified human being was dug up in New York. Known as the **'Cardiff Giant'**, the great showman P.T. Barnum had a copy made which he exhibited.

How much did the psychiatrist charge the Incredible Hulk?

£15 for the visit and £150 for the couch.

Following one of his victories, the 14th century Turkish chief Tamerlane built 120 pyramids containing the heads of 80,000 of the defeated enemy.

Research shows that over 50% of us die within three months after our last birthday. People seem to look forward to their birthday and a very low percentage die in the months leading up to this celebration.

What does Dracula take when he get a cough?

Some coffin drops.

Glad-wish Wood, Sussex, is haunted by the ghost of nineteen year old David Leany, who was hanged for a murder that it was later proved he did not commit. His last words were: 'I shall come back to haunt those people who have hounded me to my death.' He did.

Anyone who is a real witch is said to be able to hear voices in the wind. See if you have special powers by listening very carefully the next time you hear the wind howling. It might have a special message for you.

A proper witch's broomstick can be made quite simply by typing some twigs on to the end of a large can or broom stick. Such a broom is known as a 'besom'.

Anyone who has a fear of spiders will be horrified to learn that in country areas there is an average of 50,000 spiders per acre.

Why is the Dracula family so close?

Because blood is thicker than water.

Stunt man, Bobby Leech, plunged over the Niagara Falls in 1911, breaking every single bone in his body. Miraculously he survived. When fully recovered, he slipped on a banana skin on a visit to New Zealand and died as a result of his fall.

Little Willie's dead,
So jam him in a coffin,
For you don't get the chance
Of a funeral of'en.

A really spooky game, especially if played in the dark is 'The Ghost of the Cave'. In a ghoulish voice that would chill anyone's blood, you say to your friend: *'I am the ghost of the cave, and I'm coming to haunt you tonight, Sarah. Sarah, I'm on your one step.* (Make your voice even more ghostly.)
Sarah, I'm on your two step.
Sarah, I'm on your three step.
Sarah, I'm on your four step.
Sarah, I'm on your bedroom door.
Sarah, I'm at the foot of your bed.
Sarah, I'VE GOT YOU!'
You can keep this game going for a long time, the point being to create an element of surprise so that your victim doesn't know when you are going to shout *'I've got you!'*.

At Marnhull in Wiltshire, in the dead of night, two ghosts walk through the night, bearing a coffin. Their faces are never seen, but they are probably victims of the plague as the bodies of many plague victims have been discovered in this area.

Whilst investigating factory conditions American writer, Upton Sinclair, saw that dead rats were swept onto a conveyor belt and eventually ended up in some sausages, and that two workers who accidentally fell into a vat came out as pure lard. That was in 1906, fortunately conditions have changed!

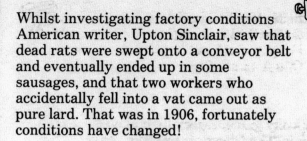

'When I got on the scales this morning I weighed eleven kilos.
'Your scales can't be very accurate.'
'Yes, they are — all I had to allow for was the fact that the needle had gone round twice.'

More than 1,000 children were kidnapped in the early seventeenth century and were shipped to America as slaves.

In 1899 thousands of people went on a day trip to Georgia to witness a lynching. The poor victim's heart was cut in little pieces and sold as souvenirs.

At Beaulieu, Hampshire, the ghostly foot-steps of Mary, Queen of Scots, can be heard running down the stairs of Palace House in the middle of the night as she re-enacts her escape.

What did the little girl say when she saw the ghost of Charles I?

'You must be off your head.'

When I die, bury me deep,
Bury my history book at my feet.
Tell the teacher I've gone to rest,
And won't be back for the history test.

An ancient cure for many illnesses was to let the patient bleed for a while. This was known as 'blood letting'. Unfortunately some doctors tried to let out more blood than the human body is known to contain. They lost their patients!

Anne Hinchfield, a twelve-year-old girl, continued to haunt her former home in Ealing for over 50 years after her death. A photograph taken of the empty house just before it was knocked down shows the wraith-like figure of a young girl at one of the windows. Was it Anne Hinchfield?

How does a ghost look when it is worried?

Very grave.

The Manor House at Sandford Orcas, Dorset, is haunted by no fewer than fourteen ghosts, including a gentleman farmer who hanged himself in the early eighteenth century. When a group family photograph was taken on the lawn in front of the Manor in recent years, the ghostly farmer appeared quite clearly in the picture too.

'Mad Monk' Rasputin was assassinated in 1916. He was first fed poisoned cakes and wine, was then hit on the head with a lead pipe, and was then thrown into the river. A post mortem revealed that he had died of drowning.

At Seafield Bay, Suffolk in the dead of night the screams of witches can be heard. These ghostly cries linger from the days when witches were tortured to death by the Witch Finder General.

*There was an old lady of Worcester
Who was kept awake by a rooster.
So she chopped off its head
And made sure it was dead,
And now it can't crow like it use-ter.*

In the fifteenth century, the Turks used special guns to terrorize their enemies. They were so large that it took one hundred men to load and fire one gun.

The village of Buxted in Sussex is
haunted by Nan Tuck, a woman who was
branded a witch. The villagers attempted
to drown her in the pond, but she escaped
and was later found hanging in a nearby
wood. Today her wraith has been seen
running towards the church along Nan
Tuck's Lane.

In a 500 year period in Germany, between
the thirteenth and eighteenth century,
more than 100,000 people were killed
because they were suspected of being
witches.

The murder rate in the United States of
America is 250 times greater than in
Japan. In Japan it is illegal for an
ordinary person to buy a gun.

Sir Piers Leigh was killed at the Battle of
Agincourt in 1422, and at his wish his
body was brought home to Lyme Park,
Cheshire, for burial. For centuries later a
ghostly funeral procession was often
witnessed, taking Sir Piers to his final
resting place. In recent years nothing has
been seen of the spirit procession, other
than one lone mourner walking with her
head bowed.

Why couldn't the skeletons go to the disco?

They had no body to go with.

Up until 1823, the bodies of suicides were buried at crossroads with a stake through their heart to prevent them from rising and haunting the neighbourhood.

French politician, Jacques Necker, had his dead wife's body placed in a large stone coffin filled with alcohol to preserve her. He visited the corpse every day.

'Doctor, doctor, I keep thinking I'm a ghost.'

'I wondered why you just walked through the wall.'

In Baltimore, Maryland, there is a convicted murderer called Ima Lyre.

The ghost of Polly Nichols has frequently been seen as a huddled figure lying in the gutter in Durward Street, London. Polly was the first victim of that Victorian horror, Jack the Ripper.

Every King of England to bear the name Richard, of which there have been three, has each died a very violent death. Since King Richard III was slaughtered in the Battle of Bosworth Field, no monarch has taken the name Richard.

Willie, with a thirst for gore,
Nailed his sister to the door,
Mother said with humour quaint:
'Now, Willie dear, don't scratch the
paint.'

What kind of ship did Dracula captain?

A blood vessel.

Who is murderous and comes from the North Sea?

Jack the Kipper.

Edward VII is the only king of England to have played the part of a corpse on stage.

Gyles Brandreth, the author of **1000 Horrors**, has never seen a ghost, but his sister Hester has seen two. One was the ghost of a young soldier killed in the Second World War, the other was the ghost of a cat called Griggs. How many ghosts have you seen?

If you would like to receive a newsletter telling you about our new children's books, fill in the coupon with your name and address and send it to:

Gillian Osband,

Transworld Publishers Ltd,

Century House,

61–63 Uxbridge Road, Ealing,

London, W5 5SA

Name ....

Address ....

....

CHILDREN'S NEWSLETTER

All the books on the previous pages are available at your bookshop or can be ordered direct from Transworld Publishers Ltd., Cash Sales Dept. P.O. Box 11, Falmouth, Cornwall.

Please send full name and address together with cheque or postal order—no currency, and allow 45p per book to cover postage and packing (plus 20p each for additional copies).

WRITE YOUR OWN HORROR STORY